MANAGE YOUR

MONEY

Leo Gough

TEACH YOURSELF BOOKS

British Library Cataloguing in Publication Data.

Gough, Leo
Managing your money. – (Teach yourself)
1. Finance, Personal
I. Title
332'. 024

ISBN 0 340 67000 2

First published 1996
Impression number 10 9 8 7 6 5 4 3 2
Year   1999   1998 1997

Typeset by Transet Limited, Coventry, England.
Printed in Great Britain for Hodder & Stoughton Educational, a division of Hodder
Headline Plc, 338 Euston Road, London NW1 3BH by Cox & Wyman, Reading, Berks.

CONTENTS

INTRODUCTION

People are eccentric about their money. This is not surprising, considering how large a part money plays in all our lives. What is surprising, though, is how bad most of us are at managing our money. We wouldn't expect to be able to function very well in the world if we didn't know how to read, but we aren't taught the basic skills of money management at school, and unless we were lucky enough to have been brought up in a family which was 'good at money', we have to develop this ability by trial and error.

Money matters generate a lot of emotion. When you don't have the skills, it is hard to keep control of your money, and very easy to get upset about quite minor money problems. This book will introduce you to the skills you need to cope financially. By applying a few basic principles you will develop abilities you may never have thought you had – hopefully, money problems that once seemed ominous and insurmountable will become straightforward matters. If you learn to become a good money manager, there is no reason why you should not achieve prosperity; perhaps you will even become rich!

We live in a bureaucratic world, and in order to flourish we have to learn its rules. Topics such as insurance and pensions can seem very boring, which is probably why many of us don't learn anything about them until we absolutely have to. Nor is it easy to imagine anyone wanting to understand how the state benefit system works unless they know they are going to make a claim. Nevertheless, these topics and others do affect you, if not now, then at some other time in your life. Learn how these systems work, and don't just rely on what you hear from friends and acquaintances. They may know about the parts that affect them personally, but they probably can't give you a balanced picture, which is what you need.

In developed countries such as the UK, people's financial behaviour can be said to divide them into three main types.

1. Floaters – these are people who, whether or not they have a job, don't feel inclined to plan for the future. They prefer to rely on things working out by themselves and tend to spend everything they earn as soon as it comes in.

2. Earners and spenders – these are people who get well-paid, but borrow a lot. Maintaining a lifestyle a little beyond their means becomes all-important, and most of their salaries are used for this purpose. This can lead to problems if they lose their jobs, or after retirement.

3. Planners – these people set their goals carefully and save systematically in order to achieve them. They think about possible problems well in advance, and take steps to prepare for them. They know that they can get rich slowly by persevering.

Of course, there is a bit of all three types in most of us. This book is about becoming a planner, because it is the most powerful way of dealing with money. Planning is just a matter of developing good financial habits. Training yourself to have good money management habits to the point where they become effortless and natural will definitely help you to become more financially secure in the future.

Never let anyone tell you that you'll never be any good with money. If you try hard enough, you can become one of those admirable people, a capable money manager. I hope that this book helps.

1

TAKING CHARGE OF YOUR MONEY

With the average annual salary at around £17,000 per year, and the average working life still thought to be 40 years, it is likely that £700,000 will pass through the average worker's hands during their lives. The ultimate object of good money management is to make some of this money stick to your fingers!

In this chapter we will look at some of the basic principles of money management:

- Dealing with a changing system
- Eight rules of good money management
- Taking stock of your situation
- What are you worth?
- What is your net worth?
- Reducing your liabilities

— Dealing with a changing system —

While the basics of money management never change, everyone needs to have an idea of what is going on in the world around them. In the last 15 years there have been dramatic changes in the way money is handled, and these changes are still going on.

- It is recognised in international financial circles that, for complex economic reasons, no country will be able to provide complete state health, education and pension services in the future. The trend is towards individuals in society concentrating on 'self-help' – in other words, we will increasingly be expected to pay for these services out of our savings and insurance. However laudable or iniquitous you personally feel this trend to be, it certainly exists, and it is important to recognise that it is not just happening in the UK; this is a world-wide trend.

● Drastic changes in the financial services industry means that there is a lot of uncertainty about matters such as banking, insurance, mortgages and so on; the kinds of financial facilities that are available to you now are more sophisticated than they have ever been. These changes make it important to seek specialist advice before you take any big financial decisions (see Chapter 4). You should not simply hand over responsibility for your affairs to an adviser, however; you need to have enough knowledge yourself to make your relationships with your advisers work properly.

Eight rules of good money management

Despite all the changes, the essentials of handling money will always stay the same. Here are the basic principles.

1 Don't spend more than you earn. This is easy to say, but hard to put into practice, especially if you have been used to spending what you earn as you go along, and borrowing a bit more as well. What it really means is that if you get out of debt and start putting aside part of what you earn, you will gain much more control over your financial destiny.

2 Make sure that you have a budget and use it as a tool. This is simple housekeeping.

3 Clear your debts. It is fairly easy to borrow money, but harder to pay it back. By getting control over your borrowing you will save a lot of money in interest and charges.

4 Save up a cash deposit to cope with unexpected emergencies. Aim to have three quarters of your annual gross salary or 10% of your net worth (see page 13) in an account which you can draw on at any time.

5 Always read the small print of any agreement. If you fully understand what you're agreeing to, you will know what to do if something goes wrong.

6 Take the trouble to seek redress if an organisation doesn't keep to an agreement. Any organisation which deals with consumers is

heavily regulated; if you think that you have not been dealt with fairly, make the effort to complain.

7 Do your homework. Don't rely on glossy brochures and smart sales talk for your information. If you are about to make a financial commitment, take the trouble to understand it properly before signing up.

8 Keep copies of all paperwork to do with money. This incudes bank statements, correspondence, loan agreements and bills. The main reason for doing this is so that you can check for errors and prove your case at a later date if you have to.

—— Taking stock of your situation ——

The secret of managing money is regular budgeting – it is something that we all do naturally, if only in our heads, but making it a formal exercise that you do on paper once a month turns it into a powerful financial tool.

Before you can budget properly, you need to take stock of your financial situation.

What are you worth?

This is a question you need to be able to answer accurately. You may think you have a rough idea, but until you get it down on paper you won't be able to examine all your assumptions – values change all the time, and if you aren't on the ball you can make mistakes.

Step 1

First of all, write down the values of each of your assets (cash and things that are worth money); don't be concerned if you don't have any, though by the time you have finished reading this book you will be some way down the road towards acquiring some. A list of your assets may include the following.

● Your home – write down a realistic sale value, net of professional fees, minus the amount of mortgage outstanding. If you have an endowment mortgage, there is an added complication in that the value of the endowment may not, in some cases, exactly match the outstanding mortgage; check the growth of the endowment policy with your lender.

- Your car – a realistic value you would get if you sold it quickly.
- Valuables – jewellery and other valuables at their insurance valuation (but remember, if you ever have to sell them in a hurry you will probably get much less).
- White goods – these are appliances such as washing machines and freezers. Write down what you think you would realistically get for them if you advertised them locally (this will be much less than their new price).
- Pensions – the current value of any fund you have.
- Life assurance – the surrender value of any policies.
- Savings – these may include building society deposits, bank deposits, and National Savings certificates.
- Investments – the market values of shares, unit trusts (bid price), bonds and other investments.

Now add up the total.

Underneath, note your 'expectations' – this is an old-fashioned word for assets which you expect to inherit on the death of relatives. While you almost certainly don't know the exact amount you will inherit, or when it will happen, it is sensible to asses your expectations, if you are lucky enough to have any. Don't add them to your asset total, though, because you don't have them yet.

In general, the older people get the more assets they have. If you are a student, you may for instance have a car worth £200 and nothing else with a resale value. This is nothing to worry about – the reason for assessing what you are worth is so that you can rationally decide what to do next.

Step 2

Now make a list of your liabilities. We cheated a little by deducting the mortgage from the value of your home already, but this was because the loan is directly tied to the house. If you have an endowment mortgage, put down the estimated sale value of your house and the estimated value of your policy on the assets list, and the cor responding loan on the liabilities list.

Write down all your other debts, and the rates of interest that apply (you will find the interest rates in the paperwork).

- Credit cards – each type of card, the current total due as of the last statement plus any purchase you have made since then.

- Shop debt – what you owe on storecards and accounts.
- Bank loans – outstanding amounts, plus the monthly payment and the number of months to the end of the term.
- Bank overdraft – the amount currently outstanding.
- Hire purchase agreements – the monthly payments and the number of months to the end of the term.
- Finance company loans – the payments and the period left until the end of the term.
- Informal loans – for example, from friends and relatives.

Step 3

Subtract the Step 2 total from the Step 1 total; the result is your 'net worth'. If it is a positive number, all well and good, but don't despair if it is a negative number. Most people, when starting out in life, and many people after they have gone through a major life crisis, find themselves with a negative net worth. You **can** change it to a positive number in time.

Now that you know your net worth, you have a benchmark by which to measure your progress in the future. The lists and calculations you have made are your 'balance sheet'. Write the date on your balance sheet and keep it in a file. In the future it will be useful as a benchmark to see how your financial situation has progressed.

What is your net worth?

Here are five arbitrarily drawn categories to illustrate the implications of the value of your net worth.

A Over £20,000

B Between £5,000 and £20,000

C Under £5,000

D Between 0 and £5,000 in the red

E More than £5,000 in the red

Categories A, B & C

How much of your net worth is accounted for by the net value of your home? If it is more than 90%, you need to save more cash (see page 43).

Category D

Make a resolution to turn your net worth into a positive number within a given time period – say three years or less – and write it down on your first balance sheet.

Category E

If you were a limited company and fell into this category, you would probably have to close down at once as being insolvent. Fortunately, as human beings, society gives us some protection, and as a last resort one can 'wipe the slate clean' by going bankrupt (see page 204) – this is not a soft option, but it does mean that no-one need fear being chained to heavy debts all their lives. There are many other ways of reducing debt which you should explore first – see Chapter 2.

EXAMPLE

Karen is 22 and has just left university. She doesn't own her own home; in fact, her assets consist of a second-hand car worth about £400 (she has established this by looking up the average price of models of that year in one of the car price guides on sale at newsagents and taking a lower value) and some jewellery which is insured for £600 but which she would never sell. She knows that her other possessions, such as clothes, books and a music system, have little or no resale value. Her 'expectations' are good; she is an only child and her parents own their own home, and while she doesn't know exactly what their net worth is, she has an idea that it is over £100,000. Her liabilities consist of a bank overdraft of £800, a credit card with £200 owing and a loan of £650 from her father.

Karen's balance sheet

Assets		*Liabilities*	
Car	£400	Overdraft	£800
Jewellery (insurance value)	£600	Credit card	£200
		Family loan	£650
Total	£1,000	Total	£1,650

(Expectations – over £100,000)

Her net worth is £1,000 – £1,650 = –£650.

This puts her in the 'D' category. It's nothing serious, but her overdraft and credit card are costing her money in interest, and she has no cash savings, so she will have to borrow from somewhere (perhaps her parents) if she needs cash in a hurry.

EXAMPLE

Contrast Karen's situation with Mike's, who has exactly the same list of assets and liabilities, plus a flat with a 100% mortgage on it. Unfortunately he has no expectations of inheritance. He's 30 years old and is about to start a new job after being out of work for six months.

Mike's balance sheet

Assets		Liabilities	
House (value – mortgage =0)	–	Overdraft	£800
Car	£400	Credit card	£200
Jewellery (insurance value)	£600	Family loan	£650
Total	£1,000	Total	£1,650

Mike's net worth is also −£650, but his situation is different. He has a commitment in the form of a home and a mortgage, and he is supporting himself, although he still has some support from a relative. His new job will give him a salary of £12,000 a year. He needs to pay off his credit card and overdraft within the next few months and start saving.

These examples are of people who have not got much money, but who are by no means in dire straits. Your own situation may be significantly better or worse than theirs, but the same principles still apply.

Reducing your liabilities

Most of us would benefit from reducing our liabilities; everyone likes to spend, and even if you are able to limit your spending by keeping track of your money in your head, if you don't regularly review your liabilities – say every three to six months – they may creep up without you noticing.

Here's how to conduct your review.

Look at each item on your liability list, first to see how the situation has changed since the last review, and then to see if you can reduce any of the debts.

- Mortgage – have you got a competitive interest rate? Is it worth switching? (See Chapter 11).
- Credit cards – are you allowing interest payments to pile up on outstanding balances? If so, stop using your cards and pay off the backlog as soon as possible.
- Shop debt – do you really need to have storecards and accounts? Are they encouraging you to buy things you don't really need? Do you pay them off each month or is there a backlog? Unless they are genuinely useful for some reason you should consider closing these accounts.
- Bank loans – are you able to pay part of the loan back early?
- Overdraft – can you pay off your overdraft?
- Hire purchase agreements and finance company loans – in general, these should be paid off as soon as possible, but check to see if there are penalties for doing so.
- Loans from friends and relatives – financially, this kind of loan, unless it is secured or you have signed some agreement, is the least important to pay off, assuming that you are paying no interest. Morally, however, it is arguably the most important kind of debt to repay quickly.

Reducing your liabilities is an important way of staying solvent. If you have stubborn debts that take a long time to clear, they may well be expensive in terms of interest and charges; ideally your liabilities should be a fraction of your net worth.

EXAMPLE

Let's look at Mike's situation a year later. His asset values haven't changed, except he's managed to save £300 in a building society account. On the liability side he has been able to pay off his credit card, and at several times during the past year his bank account was in the black. At the moment, though, it has crept back up to £500 in the red.

Mike's new balance sheet			
Assets		*Liabilities*	
House (value – mortgage =0)	–	Overdraft	£500
Car (hasn't depreciated)	£400	Family loan	£650
Jewellery (insurance value)	£600		
Building society account	£300		
Total	£1,300	Total	£1,150

Mike's net worth is now £150, which is a definite improvement. He still needs rainy day money, though – suppose he needs to buy another car in a hurry? He's doing the right thing, but he needs to keep going in the same direction. If he has been compiling his balance sheet regularly, he can monitor his progress closely, which will help him to keep control.

Summary

Your balance sheet is the basic tool you need for knowing where you stand financially. Draw up a balance sheet once a year – and each time your financial situation changes substantially. Make sure that you keep all your balance sheets together in a file, and compare them from time to time; they provide you with the bald facts about your assets and liabilities upon which you can base your future plans.

2

MANAGING YOUR BUDGET

In the previous chapter we looked at how to use a balance sheet to get a 'snapshot' of your true financial worth at any particular time, and noted how comparing your annual balance sheet with those of previous years tells you whether your net worth is increasing or decreasing. In this chapter we will look at how to manage money in the short term – from week to week and month to month. Budgeting is the 'housekeeping' part of money management; the aim is to make sure that you have enough money to pay your bills when they fall due, and, hopefully, have enough left over both to spend something on non-essentials, and to save.

Keeping records of what you spend

Budgeting only works if you are truthful with yourself and have all the relevant information to hand. For this reason, it is important to:

- Keep most or all of your receipts.
- Keep a note of money you spend for which you don't receive receipts; for example, if you spend a night out in pubs, clubs and restaurants, the chances are you won't have any receipts. Get into the habit of noting down what you have spent in a diary or notebook so you can refer to it later.
- Keep all your bills and bank statements.
- Keep all correspondence relating to expenditure; this includes letters from your bank, and from gas and electricity companies.

Ideally, you should be able to account each week for what you have spent down to the last few pounds or so. This is easy if you keep the paperwork organised in files, envelopes or boxes which don't take up much space and are easy to transport. Don't pile everything into one shoebox – separate it into categories so that you can find what you want easily.

—————— Drawing up budgets ——————

To budget properly, you need to draw up a rough budget for the whole of the coming year as well as more precise ones for the next month or two. Annual and monthly budgets give you your incomings and outgoings, and enable you to anticipate your cash needs. Remember to keep all your budgets so that you can compare them with previous periods.

—————— Balancing the budget ——————

Start by drawing up a list of what you spent last year; once you have done this, you can use the figures to estimate with a fair degree of accuracy what next year's figures are likely to be. People spend their money on different things, so here is a fairly comprehensive list of budget items – delete those that don't apply to you.

Last year's expenditure

Accommodation (mortgage or rent)   £

Food (including restaurants, school dinners,
    motorway sandwiches)   £

Household consumables (things you buy for the
    house, such as detergents, garden and hoover bags)   £

Bills
- Telephone   £
- Electricity   £
- Gas   £
- Oil   £
- Solid fuel   £
- Council tax   £
- Water rates   £

- TV licence £
- Equipment rental & HP £

Insurance
- Buildings insurance £
- Contents insurance £

Car
- Car insurance £
- Fuel £
- Repairs and servicing £
- Road tax and MOT £
- Loss of value (this is called 'depreciation' – for information on how to calculate depreciation see Chapter 12. £
- AA/RAC membership £

Other transport (including trains, buses and taxis) £

Savings and investment £
- TESSA £
- PEPS £
- Bank/building society deposits £
- SAYE £
- Life insurance £
- Pension £
- Other £

House maintenance £

Holiday
- Travel £
- Hotels £
- Spending money £

Other personal items
- Cigarettes £
- Alcohol (include what you spend in pubs) £
- Theatre/cinema/video £
- Sports and hobbies £
- Newspapers, magazines, audio cassettes £
- Clothes £
- Other £

Miscellaneous
- Furniture   £
- Pet food and vet fees   £
- Borrowings   £
- Other   £
- Bank interest and charges   £

Tax, if not taken at source   £

Total expenditure   £

Last year's income   £

**Your total income after tax from all sources
(including state benefits)**   £

In order to compile this list accurately, you will need to look at last year's bills, receipts, bank statements and expenditure notes. This will take you a few hours, but you only have to do it once a year.

Subtract your total expenditure from your total income. If there is a surplus, think about where it is (it might be in your bank account), and adjust the expenditure list so that total income minus total expenditure is zero. Notice that in this context expenditure includes savings and investments, which is money that you still have. This process is called 'balancing the budget' – income and expenditure are equal. Date this list of items and file it.

EXAMPLE

Ros, 25, has spent a few years travelling abroad, and returned to the UK early last year in order to pursue a career. She works as a graphic artist for a small advertising agency in a provincial town. Last year was hectic, what with settling into a new job, finding somewhere to live and getting used to UK prices again. So this year she has resolved to budget more carefully, especially because she wants to save up for a long holiday, which she wasn't able to do last year.

The first thing she does is to list her income and expenditure for last year.

Ros' total income after tax from all sources was:	£10,544

Her expenditure was:

Accommodation (rent) £60 a week	£3,120
Food (average £35 a week)	£1,820
Household consumables (average £5 a week – Ros doesn't buy much for the house)	£260

Bills
- Telephone (Ros pays about £50 a quarter) — £200
- Electricity (average £30 a quarter) — £120
- Gas (Ros has central heating, which she uses a lot, so her bills are fairly high, even in the summer) — £800
- Council tax (Ros' landlord pays the council tax, and water rates, which he partly gets back from her in her rent) — –
- TV licence (Ros deliberately doesn't keep a TV) — –

Insurance
- Contents insurance (Ros didn't insure the contents of her first flat last year, deciding that there wasn't anything of value that could be stolen) — –

Car
- Car insurance — £200
- Fuel — £500
- Repairs and servicing (Ros pays over the odds for repairs because she goes to expensive garages) — £400
- Road tax & MOT (Ros pays her road tax six-monthly) — £174
- Loss of value (depreciation) (Ros' car was a bargain at £150, and she is confident she can resell it for the same amount) — –
- Car purchase — £150

Other transport (including trains, buses and taxis; most of this money goes on train fares to visit her boyfriend) — £400

Savings & investment (Ros' employer offers no pension scheme, and Ros did not save anything last year) — –

Holiday (Ros could not find the money to go on holiday last year)	–
Other personal items	
• Alcohol (including what she spent in pubs)	£500
• Theatre/cinema/video	£100
• Sports and hobbies	£100
• Newspapers, magazines, audio cassettes	£200
• Clothes	£1000
Miscellaneous	
• Furniture	£200
• Bank interest and charges (Ros has a bank overdraft most of the time, and sometimes she goes over the limit without prior agreement. When she looks at her bank statements, she is a bit shocked to see how much it has cost her.)	£300
Total expenditure	**£10,544**

Having drawn up this list, Ros takes stock of her situation. Her salary is below the national average, but she feels that her job has a future, and that the experience she is getting will help her to get better jobs in the future. Many of her friends are on the dole, and she thinks that she has been reasonably lucky to get a job so soon after returning to the UK. She very much wants to go on holiday this year, and decides to economise a little so that she can save up for it. The categories she identifies as being candidates for economising are:

• Gas	£800
• Repairs and servicing	£400
• Other transport (including trains, buses and taxis)	£400
• Bank interest and charges	£300

Ros thinks that she may be paying over the odds for these items, and resolves to look for ways of reducing the amount she spends on them. She reckons she should be able to save at least £350, which would be enough for a cheap holiday.

─────── The annual budget ───────

Having listed last year's income and expenditure, you can draw up your budget for the coming year. Since you know, in detail, what you spent last year, you can estimate what you will spend next year. Just repeat the list of items and write down your estimates. They won't be exactly accurate, but they'll give you a reasonable idea, and will help you to focus on items on which you may want to spend more money, or less, next time. Head this list 'Annual budget', date it and file it. Once you have been doing this for a few years, you can compare the annual budget you made at the beginning of the year with the 'last year's income and expenditure' list you make at the end of the year – whether or not they match will tell you a lot about what has been going on in your financial life.

There is a blank annual budget form in the Appendix on page 206 which you can use.

EXAMPLE

Ros now draws up her annual budget for next year. She makes several assumptions.
- That prices won't rise significantly next year
- That her circumstances will not change
- That her car will keep going for another year

Ros' annual budget

Ros' estimated total income after tax, from all sources	£10,544
Ros' estimated expenditure:	
Accommodation (rent) £60 a week	£3,120
Food (average £35 a week)	£1,820
Household consumables	£260
Bills	
• Telephone	£200
• Electricity	£120
• Gas (Ros thinks she wastes money by having the central heating on when she is not at home and when it is not cold, so she thinks she should be able to cut down by £200 from last year's bills.)	£600
Insurance	
• Contents insurance (Ros decides not to insure her contents for another year)	–

Car
- Car insurance   £200
- Fuel   £500
- Repairs and servicing (Ros knows someone who does cheap repairs at home on the weekends; she is guessing, but she hopes she can cut her repair bill by £50 from last year)   £350
- Road tax and MOT (Ros pays her road tax six-monthly)   £174

Other transport (including trains, buses and taxis; Ros decides to use coaches for her visits to her boy-friend, which will cut £100 from her transport costs)   £300

Other personal items
- Alcohol (including what she spends in pubs)   £500
- Theatre/cinema/video   £100
- Sports and hobbies   £100
- Newspapers, magazines, audio cassettes   £200
- Clothes   £1000

Miscellaneous
- Furniture   £200
- Bank interest and charges (Ros realises she can cut her banking costs by staying in credit more of the time, and not going over her overdraft limit without prior agreement. She hopes to cut down by at least £100 in this way.)   £200

Subtotal   £9,744

Subtracting the subtotal from her income:

£10,544–£9,744 = £800

Ros is pleased; it looks as if she will be able both to have a holiday and to save something for emergencies as well. She knows that these are only estimates, and that she may end up spending more than she thinks, perhaps because of price increases, but she thinks she has a fighting chance of keeping to the budget. Now she can write in her estimates for:

Saving and investments   £400   *Holiday*   £400

Her total income and estimated expenditure now both add up to £10,544, so she has balanced her budget.

Cash flow

So far, so good, but annual accounting doesn't help with your day to day cash flow. To understand cash flow, you need to think about timing; your income and expenditure may balance over a year, but do they balance over a shorter period of time? In some months you will spend more than others, for example if you have to pay for car repairs, or when you buy some clothes. Most regular bills are paid quarterly, or can be paid monthly if you choose. Others, like road tax, can be paid annually or half-yearly. Sometimes it is more expensive to pay a bill monthly, so, if you have the spare cash, you will save money by paying it at a less frequent interval. An example of this is road tax, which is cheaper to pay for annually than six-monthly.

Paying most things on a monthly basis helps to even out your cash flow, especially if you receive your income on a monthly basis. If you are self-employed, your cash flow will be harder to control than if you were employed and earning the same amount, because your income won't come in neat equal amounts on the same day each month.

Your monthly budget

You could simply divide your annual budget by twelve and call it your monthy budget, but this is a rough and ready method which ignores your cash flow. To keep control of your cash flow, you need to draw up an estimate of your income and expenditure at the beginning of each month. These will include some, but not necessarily all, of the items in your annual budget.

EXAMPLE

To see why this is important, consider a month when your expenditure is high. Returning to Ros, whose monthly income after tax is £878.66, let's suppose in a particular month her estimated expenditure is £1,465.

Sample monthly budget

Ros' total income after tax	£878.66

Ros total expenditure:

Accommodation (mortgage or rent)	£240
Food (including restaurants etc.)	£140
Household consumables	£20

Bills
● Telephone (the quarterly bill is due)	£50
● Gas (the quarterly bill is due)	£190

Car
● Fuel	£50
● Repairs and servicing (Ros has a big repair bill to get her car through the MOT)	£350

Other transport	£40

Savings & investment
● Building society deposits (Ros is paying a monthly amount for her holiday and emergency fund)	£75

Other personal items
● Alcohol	£40
● Theatre/cinema/video	£20
● Sports and hobbies	£30
● Newspapers, magazines, audio cassettes	£20
● Clothes	£200

Total expenditure	£1,465

Total month's income–total month's expenditure = £878.66–£1,465
= –£586.34

Ros has estimated a shortfall of £586.34. What should she do? These are her options.

● Arrange to delay some of the expenditure to a later date.
● Pay for the shortfall out of her savings.
● Borrow the shortfall.

Let's suppose that in this case Ros doesn't want to delay any of the expenditure for various reasons, and that, while she could pay for the shortfall from her savings, she is reluctant to do so because she thinks that she would be tempted not to replace the money. This is a situation that most of us find ourselves in every few months. She is left with the last option, to borrow the shortfall. The way that many people do this is to borrow the money from the bank, as we will see in Chapter 6.

Before making this decision there is one last task to do, which is to make an estimate of the following month's expenditure, and possibly the month after that. These will be less accurate, and you can do them roughly – what you need to do is to check if there will be a surplus in those months to cover the shortfall in this one.

EXAMPLE		
Surplus/shortfall		
This month	Next month	Third month
– £586.34	£270	£320

This tells Ros how long she will need to borrow the money for – in this case nearly three months, although she can repay some of it sooner. There is a blank monthly budget form in the Appendix on page 207 which you can photocopy and use for your own budget.

Conclusion

In order to keep firm control over your budget, you need to set aside time each month to do your accounts. The tasks you need to do are:

- List your income and expenditure for the previous month.
- Draw up a detailed budget for next month, and rough ones for the following two months.
- Plan how you are going to cover any shortfall.
- If you know that there are impending costs that you hadn't budgeted for in your annual budget, refer to your annual budget and your list of last year's expenditure, and look for ways of adjusting your future expenditure.

Remember that a budget should be your servant, not your master. Don't be too rigid about sticking to your budget – if you need to spend some extra money because of an unexpected opportunity, simply re-adjust your expenditure plans.

As we saw on page 20, it is possible to smooth out your cash flow to some extent by paying many bills on a monthly or weekly basis, rather than quarterly. You often have to pay a little extra for this, however, and it may well increase both the time you need to spend on your monthly accounts and on paying the bills. Ultimately, it is a matter of taste; personally, I prefer to pay bills quarterly.

If you can train yourself to do these straightforward accounts on a regular basis, you are well on the way to mastering the art of money management.

3
MANAGING YOUR CASH

Once you have established good controls over your income and expenditure by regular budgeting, day-to-day monetary transactions become much easier. In this chapter we will look at efficient ways of managing cash and cheques.

—— Do you need a bank account? ——

In the days when people received their wages in cash at the end of each week, bank accounts were relatively rare. You had a bank account if you were rich, but if you were simply living on your weekly wages, you paid for everything in cash. The system has changed, and nowadays most people need some kind of cheque account.

To understand why this is so, think of the banking system as if it were like the road system. In a country with few roads, most people don't travel much, and when they do, they don't usually go very far. When more roads are built, industry is able to flourish and people move around much more, both for work and pleasure. People who refuse to use the new roads don't benefit from the new opportunities they bring. In the same way, a highly developed banking system allows people and companies to manage their money much more efficiently than they can in an under-developed banking system.

This is not to say that the developments in banking are all good; after all, although our economy depends on an efficient banking system, banks are not a public service – they are commercial enterprises that make profits from their customers. On balance, the benefits of having a current account outweigh the disadvantages. The main reasons are:

- Most wages are paid by cheque, and normally you will need to have an account in order to draw the money, although some payments, like benefits and state pensions, can be cashed at the post office.
- By paying regular bills and large sums by cheque, you are better protected against theft and loss than you are if you deal exclusively in cash.
- It is not safe to keep large sums of cash around the home.
- Cheque and credit card payments are recorded; this means that, for example, if a company makes a mistake and says that you have not paid a bill, you can prove that you have. Disputes are much easier to resolve if you can prove the date and amount of payments.
- Loans, transfers of money abroad and business arrangements are much easier to arrange if you already have a bank account.
- Having a bank account helps you to keep your financial affairs confidential.

Current accounts

Traditionally the province of banks, current accounts are principally intended as a convenient way of storing money in the very short term for the payment of expenses, rather than as a way of saving, although some bank current accounts now pay interest on credit balances. Building societies offer interest-bearing accounts that are, in effect, current accounts. Interest rates on current accounts are very low, relative to other types of saving account. For this reason, it is helpful to think of your current account as a place to put money for a short time; you should move any cash in the account that you don't need for paying bills in the next month or so into some form of savings account (see Chapter 5).

Opening a current account

When you apply to open a current account for the first time, the bank will want to know something about you. This is for three main reasons.

- Banks are legally required to obtain certain information from their customers.
- Banks need information about you in order to prevent fraud.
- Banks like to know your financial circumstances in order to sell you their products and services.

They require the following basic information.

- Your name and address
- Any previous name
- Your date and place of birth
- Your marital status
- Whether you own or rent your home
- The size of your mortgage if you have one
- Other bank and building society accounts
- Your occupation
- Your salary

Normally you will need to be over 18 to open a current account.

Once you have completed the form, the bank will run various checks on you. The purpose of the checks is to discover if you have ever failed to repay debts, and, in particular, whether you have had any County Court Judgements (CCJs) made against you for unpaid debts. Even if you do have a 'bad credit record', you may not be turned down, particularly if you explain the circumstances openly to the bank when you apply; it will simply mean that they are more cautious about lending you money or issuing credit cards.

What happens if a bank refuses to open an account for you?

It is a bizarre fact of life that banks sometimes refuse to open accounts for people who have never been in debt. This is because they have no credit record because they have never borrowed. If you are refused for this, or any other reason, don't despair. You should be able to find a bank that will take your business, although you may be asked to find someone to 'guarantee' your account. A guarantor agrees to repay any debt you run up using the account if you default; the best guarantor is someone who knows you well and has an account at the same bank.

Once you have had an account for a few years, you will find it easier to open other accounts elsewhere, because you will have built up a credit record.

Using a current account

Once you have opened a current account, you will be given a cheque book. You can use the cheques to draw money from banks during opening hours, and to pay bills. You may also be issued with a cheque guarantee card; this card guarantees that any cheque that you write up to a certain amount (normally £100) will definitely be paid, even if you have no money in your account. When you pay regular bills such as telephone and electricity accounts you will not need to use your guarantee card, but most businesses, such as petrol stations and shops, will not accept cheques without a cheque guarantee card. The card has a unique number, which the business writes on the back of the cheque when they accept it from you.

If the bank gives you a cheque guarantee card, it is taking a small risk. If you rush out with your new cheque book and write guaranteed cheques for £100 at every shop in the high street, the bank will have to pay them, even if you have no money in the account. In this situation, the bank would then have to try to get the money from you, which might be difficult. Because of this danger, banks sometimes refuse to give you a cheque guarantee card for some time until you have proved that you can handle your account responsibly.

When you write a cheque, always remember to fill the date, amount, and name of the payee in your cheque book as well as on the cheque so that you have a record.

The bank will normally also issue you with a cashcard (which may be combined with the guarantee card); this enables you to withdraw money from cash machines outside banking hours. If you use cash machines belonging to other banks which accept the card, you may be charged a little extra for this.

The main thing to remember when you are getting used to using your current account is that the money you withdraw, whether in cash or by writing cheques, needs to be covered by money that you have already paid in, or by an agreed overdraft limit (see page 33). If you go over your overdraft limit, if you have one, or go 'into the red' (pay out more money than there is in the account), there will be extra charges to pay, and the bank will be on its guard. Keeping control of these payments takes a bit of practice, because there are several factors which make it difficult to know exactly when credits and withdrawals occur. The main source of confusion is the system for paying in.

Paying into a current account

You should check with your bank or building society exactly how long it takes for cash and cheques to 'clear' into your account after you have paid them in. Normally cash is credited to your account the next day, and cheques on the third day after you have paid them in at a bank, but this is not always the case. This means that you cannot immediately start spending the money as soon as you have paid it into your account.

EXAMPLE

John pays a cheque for £1,000 into his account, which currently has a nil balance. He has no agreed overdraft facility. For the rest of the afternoon he goes shopping, and pays out a total of £500. A few days later he gets a nasty letter from his bank saying that his account is overdrawn, that he will suffer charges and that he must pay money in as soon as possible to cover the debt. Enraged, he charges down to his branch to 'sort them out'.

What has happened is that John has forgotten that he has a standing order (see page 32) on the account to pay £80 twice a year to a sports club. The payment was made on the day after he paid in his cheque for £1,000, and this has put his account into overdraft.

Once he has found out what has happened, John should politely explain the situation to the bank and ask them not to make any extra charges. Normally the bank will agree to this.

Another point to remember is that you need to record each payment you make into the account. You can do this in your cheque book, or in a special 'paying-in book'.

Bouncing cheques

A cheque is said to 'bounce' if the bank refuses to pay out money against it. This is done at the discretion of the bank when there is not enough money in an account to cover a cheque.

Suppose you wrote a cheque out for £10,000 on your current account, which has a nil balance and no overdraft facility. If the person who you give the cheque to pays it into their account, they will almost certainly get a letter a few days later saying that the cheque has not been paid – in other words, the cheque has bounced. You will probably be charged for this by your bank.

More serious, from your point of view, are cases where you are given a cheque which you pay into your account and it subsequently bounces.

You will then have to go back to the person or company that issued the cheque and try to get your money, and if the payer is dishonest, you may not get your money. For this reason, you should always wait for a cheque to clear into your account before providing the payer with what they have paid for, unless you are confident that they have the money in their account. If, for instance, you sell a car to a stranger who gives you a cheque, don't give them the car until the cheque has cleared.

Stopping cheques

Unless a cheque is guaranteed, the person who issues it can instruct his or her bank not to pay it during the three day clearing period. You might do this if you sent someone a cheque in the post and it got lost. In such a case, you should telephone and write to your bank instructing them to stop the cheque, and send the person a new cheque. This prevents the first cheque being paid in, either fraudulently or accidentally.

Blank cheques

Sometimes people give others signed cheques which have the amount of money left blank. This is not a good practice, even if you trust the other person, because accidents can happen, and you may find that you have paid out more than you meant to.

Bank statements

At regular intervals, usually each month, your bank will send you a statement detailing all the payments into and out of the account. They usually look something like the example on page 30.

The balance column

The first figure under the 'Balance' column tells you how much was in your account at the beginning of the month; in this case, it is £500. As each payment in or out is made, the balance figure is adjusted accordingly. At the bottom, the final balance figure for the period is shown. In this case, it is '£40.00 OD'. 'OD' means 'Overdrawn' – you owe the bank £40.

EXAMPLE

Name of your bank
Your name and account number
Statement number

Address of your branch and its sort code (a number which serves as an 'address' for your branch)

All entries to 28th February are complete

Date	Particulars	Payments	Receipts	Balance
				500.00
2 Feb	Bank Giro credit		50.00	550.00
4 Feb	XYZ Ltd		200.00	750.00
12 Feb	Newbury C/P			
Date of withdrawal 11 Feb		50.00		700.00
18 Feb	WXY Ltd D/D	40.00		660.00
19 Feb	000781	700.00		40.00 OD

Total payment/receipts   790.00   250.00

The receipts column

The 'Receipts' column records the amount of each cheque or cash sum you have paid into your account during the period. At the bottom of the column, it gives you the total.

The payments column

The 'Payments' column works in the same way as the 'Receipts' column: it records the amount of each cheque or cash sum you have paid out of your account during the period. At the bottom of the column, it gives you the total.

The date and particulars columns

The 'Date' column gives you the date when the money was paid in or out of the account. This is not usually the same date as you wrote the cheque or withdrew the money, because of the time it takes for transactions to clear, as discussed on page 27.

The 'Particulars' column gives you details of each transaction. There isn't much space, so the details are fairly sparse, and sometimes it will take you a little detective work to find out what they mean. You should always check the particulars of each transaction to make sure there are no errors. Taking each of the particulars in turn:

- 'Bank giro credit' refers to a cheque you have paid into your account yourself. Check your own record of payments in to see which payment it refers to.
- 'XYZ Ltd'; this gives a company name where the company has paid a cheque into your account direct.
- 'Newbury C/P'; 'C/P' stands for 'cashpoint machine'. This records withdrawals of cash made from such machines. If you have a cash-card stolen, and someone manages to withdraw money from your account, the withdrawals will come up on your statement.
- 'WXY Ltd D/D'; 'D/D' stands for 'Direct Debit' (see page 32). This refers to a prearranged payment for which you have not issued a cheque. If you are paying for something in installments, you will probably have signed a direct debit form.
- '000781'; this is simply the number of a cheque you have written out. Check the amount against your record in your cheque book.

Errors on your statement

You should always check your bank statements carefully to make sure that the transactions match your own records. If they don't, you need to find out why. Common discrepancies include the following.

- If you pay by a card that is drawn directly from your account, double payments are sometimes made. For example, you may pay by card in a restaurant, and you find that you have been charged twice when you get your statement. In such cases you should contact your bank, who will usually be able to sort this out easily and credit your account with the second payment.
- Direct Debits can be more than you expect. This is not usually the bank's fault. Contact your bank, and then the company that presented the direct debit, for an explanation.

- Your cheques can be paid out for more than you wrote on them. Someone may have altered the amount on your cheque before paying it in. This may be fraud, and you should contact the bank straight away.

Banks do make mistakes as well, especially if you have several accounts, and they get them mixed up. These errors are quickly rectified when you contact the bank. Most errors and discrepancies are either your fault, or the fault of the person who has received the money. As long as you check your statements and act quickly, you will be able to put things right in almost all cases; if you never look at your statements, you may not pick up the mistake until it is too late.

— Direct debits and standing orders —

Both these are arrangements to make a series of payments to a person or organisation.

- A 'standing order' is an instruction you give your bank to pay sums of money on certain dates. The bank may refuse to accept it if it thinks the amount is too much for you, or that you are unreliable customer.
- A 'direct debit' is an instruction to your bank to pay sums of money to others, but, unlike standing orders, you give the payee the signed form, and they send it to your bank. This can cause problems, especially where the direct debit is worded in such a way that the payee can vary both the amount and the dates of the payments. Although companies argue that they need this freedom on the grounds of efficiency, it takes the control out of your hands, and mistakes often occur. Many companies offer you a discount if you pay by direct debit because it makes life easier for them to collect money in this way. Try to keep the number of direct debits you agree down to a minimum so that you can monitor them closely.

You can cancel either type of instruction by writing to your bank.

———— Dealing with theft ————

As banking becomes more and more hi-tech, the opportunities for mistakes and theft are increasing. Here are the main tactics you can use to minimise the risk of losing out.

- Keep your cheque book and guarantee card in separate places. Banks require you to do this because it makes it harder for forgers.
- Memorise your 'pin numbers', which are the codes for using cash-cards at cashpoint machines. Don't write down the pin numbers anywhere – some thieves are clever at finding pin numbers in address books and diaries.
- Don't leave cheque books or cards lying around.
- If you find you have lost a cheque book or a card, contact your bank immediately – there is usually an emergency number you can call outside working hours. This will limit your potential loss if it has been stolen.
- Keep good records.
- Always check your statements.
- Keep your affairs as simple as you can. If you have lots of different cheque books and cards, it is much easier to get into a muddle and suffer a loss.

Bank overdrafts

Most people don't have much trouble getting their bank to allow a small overdraft facility on their current account. This doesn't mean you should use it, though – borrowing money through an overdraft is expensive, and, as we will see in Chapter 6, there are better ways to borrow. Think of the overdraft facility as a safety net to cover you if you go overdrawn because of delays in the clearing system (see page 28).

If you go overdrawn without prior agreement, it is called an 'unautho-rised overdraft'. Banks don't like this, and will make extra charges. If you are managing your account properly, you should rarely have to have an unauthorised overdraft. Suppose, for instance, that you have to pay out a cheque that will take you to your agreed limit; the first thing to do is telephone your bank, explain what has happened and tell them when you will be paying in money to cover the difference. If you do this, the bank will normally increase your overdraft limit tem-porarily and will make no extra charge.

Another use for overdrafts is when you find that your next month's income is going to be less than your expenditure. An overdraft is a convenient way of covering the temporary shortfall, as we saw in Chapter 2 (page 22).

Banks understand human nature, and they know that sometimes people run up overdrafts which they can't pay back. For this reason, they like to keep a limit on the facility which is in line with your income. As a rule of thumb, a bank doesn't like to give you an overdraft facility of more than your monthly salary.

If you do find that you have run up an overdraft that you can't clear easily, go to your bank and ask them to convert it into a loan which you pay back at so much per month. This will be less expensive in interest than keeping it as an overdraft.

One point that many people don't appreciate is that banks can recall the overdraft facility whenever they feel like it. This can happen when your bank manager changes, or if the bank is in need of cash. You are most vulnerable to this if you have a large overdraft, or if you have not been managing your account responsibly, but it can happen to anyone. Many small businesses and self-employed people get into trouble this way. Remember that you don't have a right to an overdraft, in the way that you have a right to vote – it is a commercial arrangement between you and the bank. If it happens to you, you may have to make other arrangements to borrow money in a hurry, which is yet another good reason to keep your overdraft low and clear it regularly.

— Variations on the current account —

Many banks offer a special type of current account which gives you a credit limit in return for your promise to pay in an agreed minimum amount into the account. The idea is that this is easier than arranging an overdraft facility in the normal way. If you find it difficult to get the hang of managing a current account, this kind of account (which has brand names like 'budget account' and 'flexiplan', depending on the bank) may be helpful, but once you are practised you will probably find that a normal current account gives you more freedom.

—— Managing your manager ——

In the old days, a bank manager was someone who you got to know over a period of time. He (it usually was a man) would have a lot of information about your circumstances, and if he thought you were a responsible type, he would be quite flexible. With hi-tech banking, the turnover of staff has increased, and you could find that your manager is replaced frequently. You may find yourself having to explain your circumstances all over again each time you have a new manager.

In addition, banks are keen to sell you mortgages, insurance, pensions and other financial products. You don't have to buy anything from them just because you have an overdraft or a loan, so don't feel you can't say no.

The cosy relationship may have gone, but the principles of dealing with your manager basically remain the same.

- Always answer letters from your bank.
- Always tell your bank if you have a problem with your account as soon as it comes to your attention.
- Manage your account responsibly.
- When dealing with your bank, always have your account details and any other information to hand. This shows your manager that you are on top of things.

Most problems with banks happen when you are borrowing, or have borrowed, money. Borrowing is covered in detail in Chapter 6, but the main points to remember are:

- Come fully prepared to meetings, with all your figures.
- If you are seeking a loan, the bank wants to be sure that you can pay it back; the main way that they judge this is against your income and expenditure. Showing the manager your annual and monthly budgets, and how you can afford the repayments, is the best way to convince them to give you the loan.

It is just possible that a particular manager takes against you for some personal reason. If you suspect that this is happening, move to another branch or another bank.

Bank charges

Banks charge for their services in various ways; the main ones are:

- Interest on authorised overdrafts
- Interest on unauthorised overdrafts
- Charges for letters relating to unauthorised overdrafts
- Arrangement fees for loans

- Charges for cheque books
- Charges for extra statements
- Charges for clearing cheques

Depending on the type of account you have and the interest rates set by the Bank of England, these charges will vary. At the time of writing, many current accounts incur few charges as long as you keep your account in credit, but this can change. Interest rates are published, but banks are well known for keeping quiet about the other charges – the only way most people find out about them is when they see an amount for charges on their bank statement. When you do your annual accounts, add up how much you have paid in interest and charges over the year, and then ask your bank how these were arrived at. If you feel that you are paying too much, consider moving to a bank that is offering free banking.

Credit cards

As well as guarantee cards and cash cards, there are two types of card you will come across – payment (or debit) cards and credit cards. There is often an annual charge to hold a credit card.

- Payment cards allow you to pay for purchases without writing a cheque. They are linked directly to your bank account.
- Credit cards are offered by many banks and finance companies. These are not linked to your current account, but give you a credit limit; with some you are required to settle the account in full each month, while others charge no interest if you do this but give the option to pay in installments. Interest rates are usually high.

Credit cards are a very doubtful blessing: they are difficult to monitor, because of all the stray slips of paper that you receive when you make a purchase and which you have to keep, and also because you may not have any record of purchases you make by telephone. In addition, they make you vulnerable to professional fraudsters. Nevertheless, most people find that credit cards are occasionally very useful, so it is worth having one for emergencies.

— Telephone and postal accounts —

While not strictly a different kind of account from the point of view of interest, these types of account can give you more flexibility and convenience than traditional accounts.

Girobank offers postal accounts where you can make deposits and withdrawals by post, at post offices, which are open longer than banks, as well as at cash machines. If you stay in credit there are no charges, and the ability to post deposits makes it convenient if you can't get to a bank easily during weekdays.

Telephone banking is coming to the UK, and there will be a rapidly growing range of telephone accounts available over the next few years. They work in the same way as a normal bank account, except you can talk to the bank outside normal banking hours. This is a growth area, and at present telephone banking offers attractive deals, including free banking.

One idea that may come soon is the 'smart card'. This is a plastic card with a microchip in it. It will act as an 'electronic purse' which can be loaded with 'value' which is stored there until you use it to pay for things. You can use the card in special telephones – soon everyone will have one at home – to make deposits and withdrawals, and check balances. As with all new hi-tech products, don't be in too much of a rush to jump in – its advantages and disadvantages won't be completely clear for some time yet: remember the people who bought Philips 2000 video systems, and then Betamax, before VHS became the standard format?

4
GETTING FINANCIAL ADVICE

The Financial Services Act, which came in in 1986, has introduced a great deal of protection for the consumer. The system is based on a number of Self-Regulating Organisations (SROs) and Recognised Professional Bodies (RPBs). SROs and RPBs regulate all the different types of people you can go to for advice on money matters.

- RPBs include the Law Society, which governs solicitors, and the Institute of Charted Accounts, which regulates charted accountants.
- SROs include FIMBRA, regulating independent financial advisers', and LAUTRO, which regulates insurance companies and unit trust companies.

Only ever go for professional financial advice to someone who is a member of an SRO or an RPB – this is your first line of defence should anything go wrong.

— The range of financial advisers —

The range is very wide, partly because no single adviser can be an expert in all financial matters, and partly because there is a good deal of money to be made out of giving advice. The fact that an adviser makes money should not deter you – if the advice is really good, it will be worth the cost. Not every adviser is really good, though; some are little more than inexperienced salesmen with not much training.

Since there are so many specialist advisers, it is a good idea to develop an ongoing relationship with several different ones. This way, you can build up a better picture of the overall approach to take, and benefit from their different areas of expertise.

Here are some of the main advisers you are likely to encounter.

A quick guide to financial advisers	Tied or independent?	Primary expertise	May also have	Possible fault
Independent financial advisers	Independent	May have other professional qualifications and expertise	A genuine talent for advising	Inexperience/ lack of ability
Accountants	Independent	Usually in taxation	Wide business experience	Narrow view
Solicitors	Independent	Some aspect of the law (find out which aspect)	A sophistication about contracts	Overcautious, slowness, expense
Bank managers/ Building society managers	Tied	Credit risk	Good advice on how to borrow	Too keen to sign you up
Insurance company representatives	Tied	Their own company's insurance products	A good understanding of insurance	Too keen to sign you up
Insurance brokers	Tied or independent	Insurance generally	A very good knowledge of how to ensure that genuine insurance claims get paid in full	Too keen to sign you up

Fig 4.1

Tied agents

Tied agents represent a company, most often an insurance company, and only sell the products offered by that company. They don't have to tell you how much commission they are making, but they do have to tell you that they are tied. High street banks and most building societies are tied agents. Tied agents are backed by large companies, so they are unlikely to go bust, and they may, sometimes, be able to give you the best deal on a particular product. Never sign an agreement that includes a penalty clause where you have to pay a tied agent a sum of money if you allow an insurance policy or a mortgage to lapse.

Independent financial advisers (IFAs)

These are people who may or may not have an impressive set of qualifications; the only professional qualification that they must have is the Financial Planning Certificate. IFAs have to tell you all about their charges and commissions, and must give you the best independent advice they can. IFAs may either charge you a fee for their advice, or take a commission from the company from which you purchase a product. If you pay a fee, ask the adviser to rebate any commissions to you.

Accountants

Not all accountants will give advice, but those that do are IFAs. Their great area of expertise is usually taxation, but check their qualifications and experience closely. Experienced accountants may know a great deal about business in general.

Solicitors

These will also be IFAs. Their area of expertise will be in certain aspects of the law, and you should try to find out which aspects these are. As a rule they are a cautious breed and don't necessarily know much about business. They have a tendency to charge highly for their time, and to take a lot of time.

Bank managers

Gone are the days of the wise old bank manager who knew all his customers intimately. Nowadays, you are more likely to find that your 'personal account manager' changes every year or two. They are tied agents and under pressure to sell you a host of financial products. Their area of expertise is in lending and cash flow; if you are thinking of borrowing, it is worth hearing what they have to say, even if you go somewhere else to borrow.

Building society managers

Most of these are tied. Building societies are becoming more like banks every day. Their area of expertise is mortgages.

Insurance company representatives

These are tied. They should know their own products backwards and are able to explain what is a complicated subject clearly. Don't sign up for anything without getting opinions from other kinds of advisers first.

Insurance brokers

These may be tied or independent. The good ones know a great deal about the ins and outs of different insurance companies, and, even more importantly, how to make sure that the companies actually pay out if you claim, which depends a great deal on the wording of the policy and the information that you give when you take the policy out.

Questions to ask your advisers

These may seem extremely cheeky questions, but it is your money, and you have every right to ask them. Try to get the answers to all of these in writing.

- Are you an independent adviser or are you tied?
- Which regulatory body are you authorised by? Are you fully authorised?
- Will you refer me to satisfied customers who I can ask about the quality of your service?
- Do you have a professional indemnity insurance? With what company? (This insurance will pay out claims if you have to sue the adviser for some reason.)
- How long have you worked in the advice industry and what companies have you worked for in the last ten years?
- What is your conduct record with your regulatory body? Have you ever been interviewed by them on disciplinary matters?
- Are you an agent for any financial service company, and if so, who?
- What will be your commission, if any, on the transactions you advise?
- What are your charges in detail?

- What is the risk to my money?
- Why are you advising me to do these things?
- Are you authorised to handle my cash, or do my cheques have to be made out to the company which I buy the financial product from? (The latter is probably safer even if the adviser is authorised to handle cash.)

Conclusion

In an ideal world you would develop intimate long-term relationships with two or three advisers in different fields, and conduct regular reviews with them – say, every year or two, and whenever your circumstances changed significantly. If you are fortunate enough to find advisers with whom you can do this, you will have a battery of experience and financial wisdom on your side. Getting such relationships takes effort, good judgement and time – they are like marriages, and shouldn't usually be rushed. In the meantime, take things slowly and don't sign up for long-term commitments without taking the trouble to:

- think them over carefully.
- read up on them in the financial press.
- discuss them with more experienced friends and relatives.
- make sure you understand your choices.

Remember, the more effort you put into understanding your finances, the more your advisers will be able to help you.

5

SAVING MONEY
— AND INCREASING —
YOUR INCOME

In this chapter we will look at:

- Interest
- Inflation
- Tax
- Risk
- Choosing where to save
- Bank and building society deposits
- TESSAs
- National Savings
- Increasing your income

Saving is the foundation of a secure life. In spite of housing market booms-and-busts and general economic lurches, a regular programme of saving will help pull you through.

You may feel that you need all your income just to pay your bills, but even saving a small amount regularly is enormously beneficial – try it, stick at it, and see how your feeling of financial security improves. Once you have included an amount for saving in your monthly budget (see page 20) – 5–10% of your gross income is about right when you start – you won't miss it as much as you may think.

Interest

There are two kinds of interest, simple interest and compound interest. Interest is the money you can receive as a 'rent' when you lend money to someone else; thus, making a deposit at a bank or building society is actually a form of lending. Suppose, for example, you lend a building society £1,000 at 10% interest per year. At the end of the year you will have received £100 in interest, so you will have a total of £1,100.

Compound interest

If you have lent a building society £1,000 for a year, and received £100 in interest, you have some choices. You could spend the whole lot, you could spend the £100 and leave the £1,000 on deposit, or you could leave the whole £1,100 in the account. £1,100 at 10% interest will earn £110 after another year, £10 more than if you had spent the first year's interest when you received it. By leaving all the interest you earn in the account, your savings grow faster. The table below shows how.

	Capital	Simple interest each year	Capital plus compound interest
Year 1	£1,000	£100	£1,100
Year 2		£100	£1,210
Year 3		£100	£1,331
Year 4		£100	£1,464.10
Year 5		£100	£1,610.51
Total incl. capital		£1,500	£1,610.51

Thus, after five years of reinvesting the interest, you will have earned £610.51, instead of the £500 pounds you would have earned if you had spent the interest as you received it. This may not look like much of a difference, but look at what happens after 30 years.

	Capital	Simple interest	Capital plus compound interest
	£1,000		
Year 10		£1,000	£2,593.70
Year 20		£1,000	£6,727.50
Year 30		£1,000	£17,449.40
Total incl. capital		£4,000	£17,449.40

If you had been spending the interest as you received it, you would have had a total of £3,000 interest over 30 years, but if you had reinvested it you would have earned a total of £17,449.40 (including your original £1,000). This phenomenon is called 'the magic of compound interest'. Its magic only really gets noticeable in the later years when the compounding starts to grow faster, like a snowball rolling down a hill.

Here's a more dramatic example, where you are saving a total of £1,200 a year at a rate of £100 pounds a month, with interest of 10% per year reinvested.

	Capital plus compound interest	Total paid into account
After 5 years	£9,068	£6,000
After 10 years	£27,966	£12,000
After 20 years	£151,695	£24,000
After 30 years	£328,507	£36,000

After 30 years you will accumulated the impressive total of £328,507. This is the kind of table salespeople often use to sell financial products. What they may not tell you is that the impressive effect has everything to do with compound interest and not much to do with how good their particular scheme really is.

The main point to remember is that it is better to reinvest the interest on your savings than to spend it as you receive it if you hope to increase your savings.

Inflation

As well as taxes, there is another major obstacle in the path of saving – inflation. The simplest way to describe inflation is to say that it is the gradual lessening of the buying power of currency over time.

The key points to remember about inflation are:

- No-one can predict the exact rate of inflation in the future.
- The inflation rate is fluctuating constantly.
- The official inflation rate, published regularly throughout the year, is only an approximation. The prices of the things you actually want to buy may be changing at different rates.

How inflation affects your savings

Suppose the inflation rate is 3% a year. If you kept £1,000 under the bed, in a year's time it would only have the buying power of £970 in today's money. If you deposited it in a building society at 6% interest, you would have £1,060 at the end of the year, buying power of approximately £1,028 in today's money. Thus, the interest you earn on your money will be worth rather less than you may expect, although you may still have 'beaten' inflation, depending on the difference between the interest rate and the inflation rate. In the longer term, however, inflation is likely to eat away at the purchasing power of cash deposits very severely.

Saving cash in spite of inflation

Despite the problem of inflation there are still very good reasons to save cash.

- Everyone needs cash for emergencies; it is better to use saved cash than to borrow it at consumer interest rates.
- Once you have saved up a reasonable sum, you can put it into investments that are likely to do better than inflation in the long term.
- A proportion of your net worth (Chapter 1, pages 5–7) should always be in cash or 'near cash' deposits – about 10% is reasonable – because this gives you the freedom to manoeuvre as circumstances change.

An aspect of living in a consumer society is that one can get a lot of credit to buy things. The different kinds of borrowing are discussed in more detail in Chapter 6 (page 67), but the point to remember here is:

- it is generally cheaper to buy consumer products out of your savings than to use credit.

This is because even 'interest-free' credit deals are often priced higher than equivalent deals for cash.

—— Cash-based investments ——

We are focusing on cash saving rather than investment in this chapter because it is the first basic step to getting on your financial feet. As we saw earlier, cash savings are very unlikely to beat inflation in the long term, so it is a good idea to invest in other ways when you can. These long-term investments include:

- Your own home
- A pension
- Insurance-linked schemes
- Stock market investments

Mortgages, pensions and insurance-linked schemes are covered in Chapters 11, 10 and 9 respectively. The stock market is too complicated to cover properly in this book – get a specialised book on investment to learn about it (see the Bibliography on page 216). Unit trusts and investment trusts can be relatively safe ways to invest in the stock market.

The main ways of saving cash are:

- Bank and building society deposits
- TESSAs
- Fixed-interest investments
- National Savings Certificates

The range of savings products is enormous, principally because of intense competition in the financial services industry. Some products offer guaranteed returns, while others offer variable interest rates. Depending upon economic conditions, the relative value of a savings product will change, For example, fixed interest rate deposits are attractive when the rate of inflation is low and interest rates are falling, but are unattractive when interest rates are rising, especially if the rate of inflation is high. Anyone who decides to commit themselves to a long-term programme of saving is faced with a difficult choice between investments which give the best return in the current economic conditions and those which will give a good return in a number of possible conditions which may occur in the future.

Tax on interest

In most types of account, the interest you earn is taxed. If you are a higher rate taxpayer (see Chapter 7), you will have to pay the difference between the tax which is deducted automatically from the interest and the higher rate when you pay your income taxes.

Banks and building societies usually quote two rates of interest, the 'gross' rate and the 'net' rate. The gross rate is the amount before tax, and the net rate is the amount after the tax has been deducted.

Some of the investments discussed below offer some or all the interest tax free, while others pay interest gross. Non-taxpayers can reclaim tax deducted from bank and building societies by completing an Inland Revenue claim form either when they open the account or at the point when they become non-taxpayers.

None of the savings schemes described below are subject to Capital Gains Tax (see page 77).

Risk

The first thing to consider when saving is the safety of your money. All the investment products covered in this section are considered very low risk, particularly National Savings products, which are guaranteed by the British Government.

UK bank deposits of up to £20,000 are protected by a deposit protection fund which will pay you 75% of the value of the deposit if the bank goes bust (but check that your bank is covered by the scheme – BCCI, the international bank which went spectacularly bust, wasn't). Building society deposits are protected to 90% of the first £20,000 (double this if you have a joint account). These protection schemes are actually pretty good compared with the protection offered in most other countries, so you can feel quite safe with deposits of up to £20,000. Larger sums are generally uneconomic to hold in banks and building societies for any length of time in any case, but if you must do this for some reason, consider dividing the sum into several accounts so that each one is covered by the £20,000 protection limit.

Where saving products have variable rates of interest, there is the risk that interest rates may fall and other types of investment become more attractive. This is really only a serious problem for people who need guaranteed returns; if you do need guaranteed returns, choose from:

- Time deposits
- Guaranteed bonds
- National Savings Certificates

Remember that if the rate of inflation shoots up during the period of the investment, the value of the capital will be eroded.

—— Choosing where to save ——

With the types of savings product we are examining in this chapter, your choice depends upon two essential factors.

- How long can you tie your money up for?
- How quickly can you get your money out if you need it in a hurry, and are there penalties for early withdrawal?

In general, the longer you are willing to tie up your money, and the less priority you place on early, and instant, withdrawals, the better the rates will be. Once you have decided on these points, you can then compare providers in terms of:

- The interest rates they offer for the size of the deposit you are making.
- The penalties for withdrawals.
- If there is a charge for transferring the funds to another scheme.

It is sometimes helpful to compare the net rate offered with the tax-free rate obtainable from National Savings products (see page 55).

Bank and building society deposits

Following legislative changes, banks and building societies are getting more and more alike in the range of services that they offer, and more mergers between banks and building societies are expected during the next few years.

—— Types of account ——

Current accounts (cheque accounts)

Traditionally the province of banks, current accounts are principally intended as a convenient way of storing money in the very short term for the payment of expenses, rather than as a way of saving, as discussed in Chapter 3.

Some bank current accounts now pay interest on credit balances. Building societies offer interest-bearing accounts that are, in effect, current accounts. Interest rates on current accounts are very low relative to other types of saving account, so they are not the place to put savings.

Type of account	Relative interest	Minimum	Notice for withdrawals
Current	Low or none	None	None
Instant access	Low	Often £1; higher interest if you deposit more than £500	A few days for large withdrawals
High interest	Higher	Tiered interest rates	30 or 90 days
Fixed term deposits	Highest	Tiered interest rates	90 days to several years

Fig 5.1

Instant access interest-bearing accounts

Instant access accounts can be opened with a minimum deposit of as low as £1. If you have £500 or more in such an account, the interest rate can easily be three times that of current account interest rates. Usually it is possible to make withdrawals at will, though a few days' notice may be required for withdrawals of large amounts. Often higher interest rates are offered for larger deposits on a tiered system, so, for example, you may get increasingly better interest rates the larger your balance.

High interest accounts

Both banks and building societies provide high interest or notice accounts. These accounts provide higher interest rates to depositors prepared to give notice of their intentions to make withdrawals. Periods of notice may be 30 or 90 days, although 90 days is the most common period. The longer the notice period, the higher the interest rate. Depositors who withdraw money from notice accounts without giving the agreed period of notice lose interest for the period of notice on the amount withdrawn. To attract business, the provider may allow one or two withdrawals per year without notice, fixing a maximum withdrawal amount and a minimum deposit amount. Other providers offer instant access on deposits over a certain amount, say £10,000, and require notice for withdrawals from smaller accounts.

Fixed deposits (time deposits)

These give a yet higher rate of interest, but you must tie up your money for a given period, agreed in advance. Periods vary from three months to several years, and you will generally get more interest the longer the period you agree to. Traditionally, banks have offered guaranteed interest rates for this kind of deposit, while building societies have tended to express the time element in their rate as a bonus in addition to the rate offered on notice accounts. As with high interest accounts, interest rates are tiered according to the size of the minimum deposit. If you are saving up the deposit for a house, and you know you aren't going to touch the money before you are ready to buy, then fixed-term deposits may well be worthwhile.

Regular income accounts

These are accounts which are designed for savers who want to with-draw interest regularly, say monthly or quarterly. The accounts can be either high interest or notice accounts, but with a slightly lower interest rate to compensate for the regular withdrawals. If you have enough cash on deposit to make the interest it earns a significant part if your income, you really should consider investing it in another way, to protect against inflation.

Save as you earn (SAYE) schemes

SAYE schemes are available in association with company share option schemes. In these schemes, employees save a fixed monthly amount not exceeding £250 per month for either five or seven years. At the end of a five-year scheme a bonus equivalent to nine months' contributions is added to the savings account. At the end of a seven-year scheme the bonus is the equivalent of eighteen months' contributions. At the end of either scheme the total can be used to buy shares in the employing company at a discount to their market price when the scheme began.

—— Choosing an account ——

Owing to the wide range of accounts on offer, savers need to monitor developments in their minimum deposit and interest rate structures. Every weekend the quality press publishes lists of the highest interest rates available for the major forms of deposit account, showing annual interest rates and their net value to investors liable to different tax rates.

The highest rates are normally paid by smaller building societies, who represent a slightly higher level of risk than their larger competitors. Special facilities offered on some accounts may be more important to a particular saver than obtaining the best rate. Every time a new type of account is launched, existing account holders should check to see if they would be better off closing their old account and opening a new one.

In general, banks change their interest rates more frequently than building societies do. Unless you are a keen follower of interest rates and the economy, choosing the right deposit account can be a chore – most of us aren't very good at knowing how long we can tie up our cash savings for, and penalties for early withdrawals can cancel out any benefits you might have got from a slightly higher interest rate. A practical solution is to:

- Have a current account or a combined current/deposit account.
- Save up to a few thousand (say £5,000) in a deposit account of some kind as emergency money. The difference in interest rates won't make all that much difference to what is a relatively small sum, and once it has grown above this level, you will get a better deal elsewhere.
- Not worry too much about relative interest rates, but check charges and penalties carefully before committing yourself.

TESSAs

Banks, building societies and incorporated friendly societies can offer tax-exempt special savings accounts, known as TESSAs. These were launched in 1991 for everyone over 18. Married couples can each have a separate TESSA. If you keep to the rules, the interest on the account is free of tax, but if you break the rules, the interest will suffer tax at the investor's highest rate for the fiscal year in which the breach of the rules occurs.

When TESSAs first became available, they had enormous appeal because most interest rates offered a real return above inflation, and TESSAs offered an exceptional return. By late 1993, the fall in interest rates generally meant that even TESSAs were being closed in order for capital to be moved into risk investments with potential for higher growth.

TESSA rules

The main rule is that the capital deposited must not be withdrawn for five years. The net interest can be withdrawn without penalty during the five-year period. If you withdraw more than the net interest, the account loses its tax-free status. Thus, if the basic rate of tax is 25%, a TESSA holder cannot withdraw more than 75% of the interest from the account without breaking the rule.

The maximum amount that can be invested in a TESSA over five years is £9,000. Up to £150 can be invested on a regular monthly basis, or deposits can be of irregular amounts to suit the saver's convenience.

However, not more than £3,000 may be invested in the first year and not more than £1,800 in each of the other four years. An investor who deposits less than the maximum amount in any one year cannot make up that amount by exceeding the maximum in future years. Most providers set a minimum deposit, but this can be as low as £1.

TESSAs usually pay much more attractive interest rates than normal bank and building society rates for the same amount of capital. However, the interest rate is variable. After five years, the TESSA matures and loses its tax-free status. The investor can either withdraw the total investment tax free, or leave the money in the account, where whatever interest the provider pays thereafter will be liable to income tax at the investor's highest tax rate(s).

When the TESSA matures

When the TESSA matures, the investor is allowed to replace it by a new TESSA with its own five-year term. Originally, the rules for the second TESSA were identical to those for the first. For example, the maximum deposit in the first year would be £3,000 and the total invested over the whole of the second five-year period £9,000.

However, the danger of large capital outflows from building societies when the first TESSAs matured in 1996 was such that these rules were changed in the November 1994 Budget. As the TESSAs mature, investors will be allowed to transfer all the capital they invested in their first TESSA into a new one, but they will not be allowed to transfer the interest earned on the first TESSA into the second. Thus, people who invested the maximum amount in their first TESSA will be able to open a new TESSA with £9,000 instead of £3,000. However, they will not be able to deposit additional amounts into their TESSA over the next five years.

People who invested less than £9,000 in their original TESSA will be able to add to their initial deposit over the next five years until the maximum allowed for each stage under the rules is reached. None of the foregoing applies to people who are investing in TESSAs for the first time.

Transferring a TESSA

Deposits can be transferred from one provider's TESSA to another with higher interest rates. Some providers charge a penalty for transfer, examples of which include a flat fee of £25, a loss of one month's interest or a loss of 90 days' interest. Such penalties are often associated with above-average TESSA interest rates.

Feeder accounts

Many providers will open separate accounts for up to the £9,000 maximum investment. This account will earn interest at normal (taxed) rates, and 'drip feed' money into the TESSA on the due dates for each annual installment. Transfer of a TESSA is much more likely to attract a penalty when associated with a feeder account.

National Savings products

National Savings products range from those that accept small savings to those that accept lump sums of up to £250,000. Some products enjoy generous tax concessions that make them especially attractive to higher rate taxpayers, while others pay income gross, which is convenient for non-taxpayers. The rates and range of the products frequently change, and you can get up-to-date information about what is on offer from post offices or from the Department for National Savings.

The main products are:

- Certificates
- Capital bonds
- Income bonds
- Investment and ordinary accounts

Certificates

National Savings Certificates provide a guaranteed rate of return at the end of five years. After five years, you can take the proceeds tax free, keep the matured certificate in force or reinvest the proceeds in a later issue of certificates. Certificates kept in force after five years receive interest at the 'general extension rate', which is a much less attractive rate. Certificates are issued in any amount above a minimum holding of £100, with a maximum of £10,000. With special permission, the maximum can be increased by up to a further £20,000, provided from the reinvested proceeds of matured National Savings Certificates. Interest is payable every three months.

As interest rates change, the existing issue of certificates is withdrawn from the market and is replaced by a new issue. In January 1995, the current issue was the 42nd, and guaranteed 5.85% per annum tax free. For a 40% taxpayer, this is equivalent to a taxable interest rate of 9.75%.

Capital bonds

National Savings capital bonds can be bought in any amount above a minimum of £100, with a maximum bond-holding £250,000 per person. Each bond provides a guaranteed rate of interest provided that the bond is held for five years. The actual rate of interest depends on interest rates at the time that the bond is issued. For example, a gross guaranteed interest rate on a capital bond, series I, available in January 1995, was 7.75%. The interest is not paid out but reinvested in the bond to increase its capital value. At the end of five years, the investor receives a return of the initial capital investment plus the accrued interest. The interest is paid gross but is not tax free. Interest is added to the capital at the end of each year. However, in the early years the rate of interest credited is lower than the guaranteed rate. Thus, people who surrender bonds in less than five years receive significantly less interest – none at all if the bond is encashed in the first year.

Children's bonus bonds

Children's bonus bonds are a kind of capital bonds as investments for the benefit of children under 16. They provide guaranteed rates for each of a series of five-year periods until the child reaches the age of 21 and give high interest rates, tax free. The maximum investment is limited to £1,000.

Income bonds

National Savings income bonds are designed for people who want a monthly income from their capital. The minimum investment is £2,000 and the maximum total holding is £250,000. The rates of interest are not guaranteed and are higher for deposits of £25,000 and above.

Interest is credited daily to the bond, and you can make monthly withdrawals of the interest once you have held the bond for six weeks. Interest is paid, without deduction of tax at source, into your bank or building society account on the fifth day of each month.

You can withdraw the capital in multiples of £1,000 provided that you give three months' notice. If you make withdrawals within the first year, only half of the published rate of interest will be paid. After one year, full interest is allowed up to the date of withdrawal.

Cashing certificates

If you cash a certificate within the first year, you will not normally receive any interest. An exception is if you bought the certificate with the maturity proceeds of an earlier certificate; in this case, interest would be payable. If you cash in a certificate between the end of one and five years, the interest you receive is much reduced, but is still tax free.

Inflation-hedged certificates

'Index-linked' certificates give you a guaranteed rate of interest over five years and, in addition, they index-link the capital sum invested to the Retail Prices Index (RPI). This means that if the guaranteed rate is, say, 3.5% and the annual rate of increase of the RPI is 4%, the overall return on the certificate would be 4% + 3.5% = 7.5%. In January 1995, the 8th issue of index-linked certificates were available at 3% over RPI.

The minimum holding is £100, and the maximum is £10,000. A further £20,000 can be reinvested from the proceeds of matured certificates.

The rules on first-year encashment are the same as for ordinary certificates. After one year, the index-linked return only is payable, and from the second year onwards, interest is payable, less a penalty which gradually reduces as the certificate reaches maturity.

Investment and ordinary accounts

Ordinary and investment accounts are straightforward deposit accounts paying gross interest. You receive a passbook which you can use for payments and withdrawals at post offices.

The ordinary account has a minimum deposit of £10 and a maximum of £10,000. You can hold an account in joint names. Ordinary accounts offer a standard rate of interest for deposits of less than £500 and a higher rate for deposits of £500 or more.

The first £70 of interest on any ordinary account is tax free. Interest above £70 is taxable at your highest rate(s) of tax. If two people hold a joint account, the tax-free element is increased to £140.

The investment account is a one-month notice account paying variable interest at higher rates than the ordinary account. Interest is paid gross but is not tax free.

First option bonds

First option bonds were specifically designed to appeal to basic rate taxpayers. Interest is paid net. The minimum for a bond is £1,000 and the maximum total holding is £250,000.

First option bonds guarantee a fixed rate of interest for one year. At the end of each year, a new rate of interest is fixed for the next year, and you are free to encash the bond or to continue. Interest is calculated daily but is paid at the end of each year. If part or all of the bond is withdrawn before the end of the first year, interest is not paid on the amount withdrawn. From the end of the first year, the interest paid on withdrawals which you make at a time other than on the anniversary dates is half the fixed rate.

——— Increasing your income ———

It is all very well learning about managing money, but what if you simply don't have enough, however much you scrimp and save? The UK is one of the wealthiest countries in the world – surely it is possible to increase one's income a little, if not a lot.

In this section we will look at approaches you can take to try to increase your income, whatever your circumstances. Increasing your income will make it easier to pay the bills you have already got, and leave you with extra money for saving. The main ways of doing this are:

- Getting a better-paid job
- Going into business
- Active investment

Getting a better-paid job

Life is much easier if you do work that you enjoy. If you get a highly paid job that you hate, it is quite likely that either you will not do it well, and have to leave, or that it makes you so miserable that the rest of your life becomes miserable too. For this reason, it is worth making strenuous efforts to find work that you enjoy doing.

Savings summary

Type of account	Relative interest rate	Minimum deposit	Notice for withdrawals
Current	Low or none	None	None
Instant access	Low	Often £1. Higher interest if you deposit more than £500	A few days for large withdrawals
High interest	Higher	Tiered interest rates	30 or 90 days
Fixed term deposits	Highest	Tiered interest rates	90 days to several years
TESSAs	Higher	Often £1	You can withdraw up to 75% of the interest without penalty; larger withdrawals mean that the account loses its tax-free status
National Savings products			
Capital bonds	Higher	£100	No interest if you cash in in the first year; if you cash in between years 1 and 5, the interest is reduced
Childrens' bonus bonds	Higher	£100	No interest if you cash in in the first year; if you cash in between years 1 and 5, the interest is reduced
Income bonds	Higher	£2,000	No interest if you cash in in the first year; if you cash in between years 1 and 5, the interest is reduced
Index-linked certificates	Higher	£100	No interest if you cash in in the first year; if you cash in between years 1 and 5, the interest is reduced
Investment accounts	Low	£10 Higher interest if you deposit more than £500	1 month
Ordinary deposit accounts	Low	£10 Higher interest if you deposit more than £500	A few days for larger withdrawals
First option bonds	Higher	£1,000	Full interest on withdrawals on anniversary dates; less interest at other times

Fig 5.2

If you enjoy your work, you tend to do it well. People pay more for quality, so if your work is of a consistently high standard, you will always have an advantage in the labour market. It is a positive cycle – if you enjoy your work you will do good work, and there will be more, often better-paid work for you to do.

There is one trap here that is avoidable: what if you are very good at, say, being a coal miner, but there is no coal mining work to do? The hard truth is that you have to do work for which there is a demand, or else you won't earn enough money.

It often takes a long time for people to find what they really want to do. You might try several completely different careers before you find the one you want, and you may, after doing the job you love for many years, find that you have to change directions because of changing demand. If this happens, don't despair – you will be able to find another way to use your abilities and experience if you look hard enough. This takes imagination and adaptability.

Training

Some people think that learning ends when you leave school, but in fact we go on learning all our lives. Getting more education and training is a very powerful way of improving your earning power. This is true for everyone, however much education you have or haven't had.

- If you are in work, grab all the opportunities you can to take any company training courses that come up.
- If you haven't taken a university degree, think about doing so. There is a wealth of advice available on how to do this as a mature student, and on what kind of course to study. It is quite an investment of your time, but statistically it will improve your chances of getting a better-paid job afterwards.
- If you have had a great deal of academic education and are 'out in the real world' for the first time, you may think that your qualifications aren't helping much. This may be because you lack vocational skills to do with a particular kind of work. In this case, think about taking vocational training courses. Many trade associations offer up-to-date training leading to recognised qualifications in their industry. From import/export to computers, there is a vocation out there that you will be able to train for.
- Vocational training is quite open; many very rewarding courses do not have heavy entrance requirements.

If you feel a little unsure about 'going back to school', don't worry! Educators understand the problems you are facing, and will help. Getting more training takes time, effort and endurance – if you are prepared to take the trouble, educators will meet you halfway.

Research the hidden job market

Only a small percentage of jobs are actually advertised on the open market. Most jobs are filled by people who are already known to the organisation, either because they already work there, or by recommendations from people the employer knows and trusts.

You can greatly increase your chances of getting a job if you look for vacancies that are not advertised. Unadvertised jobs have far fewer applicants, so there is less competition.

To do this successfully, you need to think of yourself as if you were a product that you had to sell to a customer. The main steps to take are:

1 Identify your strengths, experience and aptitudes, and compile a list of companies that are likely to need what you have to offer.

2 Find out about the people in particular firms who have the authority to offer you a job. It is worth taking trouble over this. Frequently, if you approach the wrong person, they will tell you that it is impossible, and if you subsequently find out who the right person is, you will be welcomed with open arms! Get to know as much as you can about the company before you make contact; you can do this by reading their literature, visiting their premises, reading the trade press and talking to people who have contact with the company, or even work in it. It may seem a bit brash, but it works.

3 Prepare a cv. This is incredibly easy if you are practised at it, but quite hard if you haven't done it for a while and are feeling a bit unsure anyway. There a number of ways to write a cv, and a great many books available on how to do it. In general, cvs should be short (two pages) and to the point, and it is worth adjusting your cv every time you make an approach to a company so that it emphasises the points you think they will like the most. A well-targeted cv is like a good brochure for a product – it opens the door to the customer.

4 When you make the approach, show that you have done your homework. Make it easy for the person to say 'yes' to you by anticipating what they need. A relaxed, optimistic manner helps a lot – it's no good going to an interview looking as if you are always miserable. If you are unsure about your interview skills, take a course on it.

Going into business

Self-employment is a very different way of life from being employed. It is more risky, demands more responsibility, and is potentially more rewarding. Not everybody can make a success at self-employment, but if you are one of those people that just absolutely has to have the freedom that it offers, you should definitely do it.

Many of us are in between. We can work in a job, or we can be self-employed. If you haven't been self-employed before, you should be aware that it is definitely not a soft option. Small business ownership is a high-risk venture. For example, a recent lifespan analysis by the DTI found that almost 40% of new registrations for VAT are gone within three years. Small business owners work long hours – surveys regularly report that over half of small business owners work more than 50 hours a week.

An estimate for the early 1990s suggested that almost 80% of all businesses in the UK had turnovers of £100,000 or less and the majority of these had turnovers of under £50,000. Once all the costs of running the business have been allowed for, this suggests that many small business owners will earn quite modest returns for their investments and hours worked. So, why do people go into business for themselves?

One survey found that the main reason for starting a business was the desire for independence.

Surprisingly perhaps, making money was the prime motivation for only 16% of those who were asked.

	%
Independence	36.0
Unemployment/insecurity	22.1
To make money	16.1
Saw a market opportunity	16.1
Inherited the business	3.6
Other/don't know	6.1

The survival rates of small businesses

In a survey of small businesses in service industries, it was found that just over 60% survived the period 1990–94. In other words, nearly half didn't survive. While self-employment can become a marginal type of existence, working sometimes and at other times claiming benefit, this chapter is about increasing your income, so in this context self-employment means that you are running a small business, if only to sell your own labour.

A self-employed business person works on average 9½ hours a day, six days a week. Despite this, surveys suggest that the majority expect this and are not disappointed, which is evidence that if you enjoy your work, you don't mind working hard.

Self-employment – a summary

If you are unemployed, becoming self-employed full time could well increase your income. If you are willing and able to seek employment, however, the regulatory and economic environment in the UK is more favourable to you than to a self-employed person, so employment is a better option if you simply want to increase your income. Self-employment is a way of life; remember that one survey found that only 16% said that they were doing it mainly for the money.

Active investment

Increasing your income through active investment depends on three main things.

- You need capital to invest.
- The more return on the capital, the more risk to the capital.
- You need skills, experience and talent to succeed at risky investment.

A few people reading this book will have what it takes to make money at active investment, if not now then at some time in the future. They probably know who they are. The majority of us would be better advised to concentrate on increasing our income through a career in employment, and developing money management and passive investing skills, which will ultimately result in prosperity. If this strikes you as an infuriating statement, perhaps you have what it takes to succeed in business!

6

BORROWING

In this chapter we will look at the basic principles of borrowing. Borrowing money is not necessarily a bad thing – even governments do it – but too much borrowing can be. The golden rule is: don't borrow as much as lenders are willing to offer you. Borrow only what you are sure you can pay back.

Short-term borrowing

This brings us back to the everyday problem we saw at the end of Chapter 2. What if you do your monthly budget and find that you have a shortfall of £475, but that you will have a surplus to pay it back with during the following two months? What you can do is to arrange for a short-term overdraft with your bank. The interest and possibly the charges you pay the bank for this will be fairly high, but as long as you clear the overdraft quickly it won't cost you too much.

What you should not do is to use an overdraft in order to borrow money for a long time – say more than a year. This is because, even if the bank will allow you to do it, it is an expensive way of borrowing.

Medium-term borrowing

If you are borrowing money for a year or more, it will be cheaper to arrange for a loan for a fixed period of time. Normally you will be required to pay back the loan over the period at so much per month.

The main ways to borrow	How long should you borrow for?	Relative cost in interest and charges	Secured?	Attitude of lender if you have trouble repaying
Bank overdraft	Not more than a few months	High	No	Generally willing to reschedule
Credit cards	No interest on most cards if you pay off the balance each month (except for cash)	High	No	Generally willing to reschedule
Bank loan	Try to keep it under two years	Quite high	Not necessarily	Generally willing to reschedule
Shop credit	As short as possible	Expensive	No	Not happy about rescheduling, but may do so
Credit on mail order goods	As short as possible	Expensive	No	Not happy about rescheduling, but may do so
Secured loans advertised in newspapers by finance companies	As short as possible – preferably under two years	Quite high	Usually secured on a property you own	May reschedule, but has the power to repossess your property
Mortgages on property	25–30 years ofter the cheapest	Depending on type, house form of consumer borrowing	Secured on your	Generally willing to reschedule but has the power to repossess your property
Loans from unlicensed credit brokers	Avoid these	Often the most expensive by a wide margin	Usually unsecured	Not likely to be tolerant

Fig 6.1

In order to get such a loan, especially if it is 'unsecured', you will need to show the lender that you have enough income to be able to afford to make the payments. This is where your annual and monthly budgets come in – if you show lenders these, they will be favourably impressed, especially if the amount you are asking for can be easily repaid out of your income. You should still ask yourself some searching questions about why you are borrowing the money, though.

Long-term borrowing

If you want to borrow money for longer than five years, the lender will generally want you to offer security for a loan. Mortgages are the most well-known example of long-term borrowing, and can be the cheapest form of borrowing you can obtain. See Chapter 11 for more details.

Secured and unsecured loans

Secured loans are loans which you agree to tie to some asset that you own. Mortgages are an example - you offer your home as security against the loan. Other types of security include:

- some insurance policies
- company shares
- valuables such as antiques and jewellery
- a legally binding guarantee that someone else (such as a relative) will pay back the loan if you don't.

In general, lenders will only lend you a proportion of the market value of the security you are offering, and prefer to lend on assets which will be easy for them to sell if you can't pay the loan back. This is the point of security – ultimately the lender has the right to sell the security to recover the money if you default on the loan.

Unsecured loans are loans which are not tied to a particular asset. This doesn't mean that you can run off with the money, but it does make it harder for the lender to get the money back if you can't pay. This makes unsecured loans more expensive in terms of the interest you pay.

Types of lending

As well as banks, there is a wide range of other organisations that lend money. The changes in recent years have brought about many mergers, so your high street bank may also have sister companies that lend in other ways. The different kinds of lending include the following.

Credit cards

These may offer a month's interest-free credit on purchases you make with the card (but not for cash withdrawals, which you will have to pay interest on right away). If you can pay off the whole debt every month, this is fine, but if you let the debt build it is an expensive way of borrowing.

Shop credit and credit on goods bought by mail order

Don't be fooled by alleged discounts in the advertising and always check the APR (see below). This is another expensive way to borrow.

Secured loans advertised in the newspapers

The advert often says something like 'pay off all your credit cards and consolidate your loan at a lower interest rate'. This is only worth doing if you really do pay off other more expensive loans with the money. Rates vary widely and you can borrow for long periods – up to 15 years or so. The loan will almost certainly be secured on your house, and, as we see in Chapter 11, the lender will not be shy about forcing a repossession if you stop paying off the loan. In general, this kind of loan is not a good idea.

Unlicensed credit broker loans

These are aimed at people who can't borrow elsewhere, and are very expensive indeed. Definitely to be avoided.

Of all the types of borrowing discussed, banks and credit cards, although expensive, are probably your best bet. This is because they are heavily regulated and have to adhere to codes of practice, so, if anything does go wrong, you can hope for reasonable treatment.

The cost of borrowing

By law, every lender has to show you the Annual Percentage Rate (APR) of interest on the loan. This helps you to compare like with like. Ignore statements like 'only x% a month' – these are quoted to make the interest rate seem lower than it really is. The APR is the rate of interest that you would pay on the loan if the interest was compounded exactly once a year (known as the 'effective interest rate') together with other charges such as documentation fees, loan fees and related charges, where applicable. When comparing the interest rates being charged on different types of loan, you should always use the APR.

As an exercise, spend an hour or two collecting examples of different types of loan on offer – look at newspaper ads, brochures that are sent to you, store credit information and brochures from banks – and compare the APRs. You will find differences of several per cent, perhaps as much as 10%, between them. This may not sound like much until you think of the much smaller variations in interest rates available to you when you save. If you could save money at more than 20% in 1996/97 (the cost of some loans) you would be doing extremely well indeed.

Is it ever better to borrow than to save cash?

Broadly speaking, during times of high inflation (in the UK, this roughly means 10% inflation or more), there can be a wide negative gap between the interest that you can get on your cash savings and the real rate at which inflation is reducing the buying power of that cash. During such times, prices tend to be increasing rapidly, and it can be a better strategy to borrow money to buy 'things', such as houses, which are increasing in value, than to keep cash which is reducing in value. Even during these times you still need to have a store of 'rainy day' cash, but this will probably be easier to come by.

For the last few years the inflation rate has been low, some prices have dropped (most notably housing prices) and the demand for cash has been high, so it has become more important for you to save cash and reduce your borrowings.

This brings us to the idea of 'gearing', which is a way of making money by borrowing when conditions are favourable.

Gearing

Gearing, or 'leverage', is a way of describing the relationship between your assets and your borrowings. The following example shows how some people make money through increasing their gearing during times when the property market is booming.

EXAMPLE

Suppose you have a house worth £100,000 and its value increases rapidly to £150,000. If you had a mortgage of £10,000, the value of your stake in the house would have increased from £90,000 to £140,000 (ignoring inflation), giving you a profit of £50,000.

Suppose that you had bought the house with a £90,000 mortgage plus only £10,000 of your own money, and that you kept the other £80,000 invested elsewhere. If the value of the house goes up to £15,000, your profit is still £50,000, but you also have the £80,000 earning money for you elsewhere.

In the first case you put £90,000 into the house to make a £50,000 profit, and in the second case you made the same profit but you only put in £10,000 – and you made profits from the £80,000 invested elsewhere.

This is a very simplified example to show the basic principle of how increasing your gearing can sometimes make you extra money. It can be a very risky thing to do, so you should only try it if you really know what you are doing.

--------------- **Conclusion** ---------------

Most people know that it is easier to borrow money than to pay it back, yet some of us seem to ignore this basic fact of life.

Here are five rules to follow when you borrow.

1 Make sure that you can pay back what you have borrowed, either out of your future income or, as in the case of houses, by the sale of an asset.

2 Don't borrow short-term money for long-term purposes. For example, even if it were possible to buy a house by taking out a bank overdraft, it would be most unwise, since you would be paying over the odds in interest, and the loan might be recalled when you least expected it.

3 Keep your short-term borrowing as low as possible.

4 Try to pay off medium-term loans early.

5 Never use borrowing as a substitute for saving. For example, it is better to save up for a holiday than to borrow to pay for it and then be paying off the loan for a year instead of saving up for your next holiday.

The famous line 'Neither a borrower or a lender be' from 'Hamlet' is much misunderstood; Shakespeare was actually poking fun at the pompous old man, Polonius, who speaks the line. We must all borrow and lend at times – it is a part of life.

7
TAX AND NATIONAL INSURANCE

It really does pay to learn something about the tax system if you want to be good at managing money. It's complicated and, if you don't already have one, eventually you will probably need the help of one of those unsung heroes, good accountants, to help you with your tax returns.

In this chapter we will look at the tax system, the main taxes and how they are calculated.

- Who is liable to UK taxation?
- How are UK residents taxed?
- Capital gains tax (CGT)
- Inheritance tax (IHT)
- The tax year
- What is VAT?
- Stamp duty
- Income tax (including personal allowances, income tax rates 1995/96 and benefits in kind)
- Filling in income tax returns (including self-assessment)
- National Insurance (NI)

The complex interaction of a wide range of taxes affects the lives of almost everyone who lives or works in the UK, together with many people who neither live nor work in the UK! As in most other countries, the taxation system in the UK is extremely intricate; if you picture each country's tax system as being a unique Heath-Robinson machine with lots of parts that don't quite make sense, it will help you to avoid the misconception which many people have that the tax systems in the UK and elsewhere are straightforward and without grey areas – ultimately they aren't, but there's no point in worrying about it.

You can probably think of the main taxes: income tax and capital gains tax (CGT). If you have experience of a relative dying, you may have come across inheritance tax (IHT) also. These are called 'direct taxes'. There are other taxes too, however, known as indirect taxes, such as:

- Value Added Tax (VAT)
- Stamp duty
- National insurance

—— Who is liable to UK taxation? ——

This may seem to be rather a strange question – isn't everybody liable? It all depends on your circumstances, and before going on to the details of how these taxes work, we should look at some basic principles.

- Residence
- Ordinary residence
- Domicile

Residence

You may be regarded as being resident in the UK in any tax year in which you are present in the UK for at least part of that time. Anyone staying in the UK for at least six months in any tax year will always be regarded as being UK resident for that tax year and, depending on the individual's circumstances, the required period could be much less then six months.

Most other countries have similar rules to these, so it is possible for someone to be regarded as being resident in more than one country in any one tax year.

Ordinary residence

Ordinary residence is a strange notion, quite distinct from residence. As it is the main criterion for CGT, it is important to get the Inland Revenue to agree that you are 'not ordinarily resident' before you make a capital gain if you want to avoid the tax. You can be resident in more than one country at the same time, but 'ordinarily resident' in only one country at a time.

A quick guide to the main taxes on individuals	Levied on	Amounts below which you pay no tax	Rate of tax
Income tax	Mainly on the money you earn from: ● employment ● self-employment ● share dividends and ● interest on government bonds	A system of allowances based on marital and parental status, and also on age (£3,525 a year for a single person in 1995/96)	After you have deducted your allowance: ● 20% on the first £3,200 ● 25% on the next £21,000 ● 40% on anything more these are called the 'marginal rates')
Capital gains tax	Mainly on 'one-off' profits	£6,000 in 1995/96; currently many exemptions and indexation allowances	At your marginal rate of income tax
Inheritance tax	The value of all your worldy goods when you die, plus some gifts you may make before you die	£154,000 in 1995/96 (the 'threshold'); can be mitigated with financial planning	40% on the value over the threshold
National Insurance	Partly a flat rate you pay each week, and partly a percentage of income	£59 per week for employers (Class 1 National Insurance); £3,310 per year for the self-employed	See page 90
Value Added Tax	Most goods and services that you buy	If you buy from a business that is not registered for VAT, you don't pay the tax	17.5%
Stamp duty	Larger house and land purchases, and purchases of stocks and shares	Houses below £60,000 in 1995/96	1% on property; 0.5% on stocks and shares

Fig 7.1

Domicile

Domicile is another strange notion, quite distinct from 'residence' or 'ordinary residence'. If you are not domiciled in the UK, you are not liable for tax except on the money that you bring into the country. There are two kinds of domicile:

- domicile of origin
- domicile of choice

Your domicile of origin is usually the country where your father was domiciled when you were born. If you have a domicile of origin outside the UK, you may be able to live in the UK for a long time without ever having to pay UK tax.

Domicile of choice is more tricky; you have to be resident in a country and have 'the intention of permanent or indefinite residence' there. If you want to change from a UK domicile, you must intend never to return for anything more than brief, infrequent visits, or the Inland Revenue will say that you haven't changed your domicile.

Each of these descriptions is used to assess whether or not you will be subject to UK taxation, or to the tax rules of another country, on:

- your earnings
- income from investments
- other sums of money, such as Inheritance Tax on death.

What if I have close connections with other countries?

If you are not a UK national, or you have a spouse who is not, or you are planning to work abroad, you should get specialist advice from a tax lawyer. You may find that you are in a position to save tax.

What is the difference between tax avoidance and tax evasion?

Tax avoidance is when you make efforts legally to reduce or avoid paying tax by exploiting the complexity of the rules. Tax evasion is exactly the same thing, except that you break the law. The right to avoid tax is well established and, to paraphrase Lord Clyde's comments in a famous tax case of 1929, a person does nothing wrong by arranging his or her affairs to take advantage of the rules, so long as they are not broken. The extraordinary complexity of tax legislation means that in practice there are many circumstances in which the lay person could not possibly tell the difference between avoidance and evasion. Nevertheless you should make sure that you do everything you can to stay within the law.

—— How UK residents are taxed ——

Earned income

If you go to work abroad for a short period of time and earn money which is paid to you in that foreign country, then you could be liable not only to the tax of that country but also to UK tax. Most developed countries now operate what are called double taxation agreements which mean that one of the countries gives up its rights to tax the individual. Usually the country in which the work is done has the right to tax that income, and your country of residence gives up that right.

For example, a UK resident who works for a short time in France will be taxed under French tax rules, and will not normally pay UK income tax on those earnings.

Unearned income

Unearned income is money you receive from investments such as stocks, shares, unit trusts, and rents on property you own. It may not seem unearned to you, but that is what it is called.

If you have unearned income from investments held in another country which does not have a double taxation treaty with the UK, you could be taxed twice. Remember, though, that most developed countries do have double taxation treaties with each other.

Suppose you received unearned income from investments in France. Because of the double taxation treaty between the UK and France, the foreign country (in this case France) will usually forego the right to tax the income, which will then be liable to UK taxation just as if that income had arisen in this country.

It is important to note that the taxation on income earned abroad by UK residents is paid when the income is earned or credited and not only when or if the money is returned to the UK.

——— Capital gains tax (CGT) ———

If you are a UK resident you are liable to CGT on gains made on the sale of assets wherever in the world they may be.

For example, if you won a villa in Italy which you sell at a profit, then you may be liable to CGT in the UK on that gain. When you calculate the profit you made on the sale of an asset, you are allowed to take the inflation of the selling price into account.

Currently, the rules on CGT are so generous that many people in the City of London describe it as a voluntary tax; this is because you can legally plan your finances in such a way as greatly to reduce CGT, or even avoid it altogether. Currently, the vast majority of capital gains that people make do not suffer any tax. At some periods in the past, however, CGT was far heavier – for instance people had to pay CGT on profits when they sold their own homes. Currently your own home is exempt of CGT, so you can keep all the profit you make. In the future, however, the CGT rules could be tightened up.

Because of the current lightness of CGT as a tax, we will not examine the rules in detail; if you are expecting to make significant capital gains (for example, if you have many properties) then you should seek help from an accountant.

In the relatively rare cases where CGT is payable, it is calculated at the highest marginal rate of income tax which you pay. The annual exemption is £6,000 for 1995/96.

What is the real difference between income tax and capital gains?

This is not always obvious, but the principle is that 'income' means your earnings, or profits on investments, which have some element of regularity. For example:

● interest earned on savings in a building society account
● salary from your job
● trading profits if you are self-employed.

Capital gains are profits made on a one-off basis which are unlikely to recur and are not profits made in the ordinary course of employment or business. For example:

- profits on the sale of an antique
- profits on the sale of a second house
- profits on the sale of shares.

In some cases, it is difficult to identify whether a profit will be liable to income tax or to CGT, and you should get specialist advice from an accountant.

Inheritance tax (IHT)

If you are either domiciled or deemed domiciled in the UK at the date of your death, then IHT may be levied at a rate of 40% on your assets, subject to a threshold of £154,000 from April 1995, wherever in the world they are situated. Like CGT, the current rules make it possible for people who are worth much more than £154,000 to avoid some or all IHT if they plan carefully with the help of professionals. Where there is an IHT liability, the effect can be very large, so it is very important for people with a high net worth to undertake financial planning in order to mitigate the liability to IHT, or at least to take out insurance policies to provide funds to pay IHT on their death.

IHT is paid on the value of assets on your death and may be levied on assets you have given away during the seven years preceding your death – it does not apply to gifts by businesses.

There is quite a number of exceptions and allowances which result in the vast majority of lifetime gifts not actually being liable to IHT, and also in the majority of estates on death also being free of IHT liability.

The tax year

The tax year, or 'fiscal year', runs from the 6th of April in one year to the 5th of April in the next. Thus the 1996/1997 tax year starts on 6 April 1996 and ends on 5 April 1997.

Most kinds of taxation are calculated on your income or gains within each fiscal year, and your residency or otherwise in the UK is taken in terms of each tax year. It is not possible to be counted as a UK resident for just three months – you either will or will not be deemed to be a UK resident for the whole of the tax year.

For income tax, your income will be calculated for the tax year, taking into account your personal allowances (see page 81) and the bands of income which are taxed at different rates.

For capital gains tax, your gains in any one tax year are totalled when deciding if there will be any liability to pay CGT for that year.

What is VAT?

VAT is added to the basic selling price of most goods and services in the UK, although there is a number of situations where VAT is not levied, in particular where the goods themselves are exempt from tax, or where the vendor (the person selling the goods) is not registered for VAT because they have a low turnover. This is why you can save money by buying the same product from a small business which is not registered for VAT rather than from a large one.

VAT affects us greatly; the higher the rate of VAT (it is currently 17.5%) the more expensive it is to buy things. In turn this leads to an individual's income having a diminished purchasing power. Ultimately this may affect your ability to save and invest money. Changes in the rate of VAT have a direct effect on inflation.

Stamp duty

Stamp duty has been removed from many transactions to which it used to apply, but is still levied on:

- the purchase of stocks and shares at 0.5%
- the purchase of land or buildings, at 1%, where the purchase price is more than £60,000.

In the case of house sales, the stamp duty is usually collected by the solicitor acting for the purchaser.

Income tax

The schedular system of income tax

For different kinds of income, in particular the distinction between earned and unearned income, there are various 'schedules', lettered from A to F, depending on the nature and source of the income.

Schedule A

This covers income from land and property, usually income from leases.

Schedule B

This used to be for income from the management of woodlands, but is now no longer operative.

Schedule C

Interest on government bonds (gilts). This is paid net of basic rate tax, but this can be reclaimed by non-taxpayers. Higher-rate taxpayers must pay the additional tax due at 15% (being the difference between the standard and higher rates of tax). This is accounted for in your tax assessment.

Schedule D

This schedule is subdivided into cases. Cases I and II relate to self-employed earnings (see page 91).

Schedule E

This is also subdivided into cases, the most important of which is Case I which relates to income from employment; this is taxed under PAYE (pay as you earn), which basically means that the employer calculates the tax liability of his or her employees, taking into account each person's personal allowances, and deducts the tax from the gross weekly or monthly salary before sending the tax to the Inland Revenue.

Schedule F

This applies to dividends paid by companies to shareholders, most often by companies listed on the stock exchange. Like Schedule C, income under this schedule is deemed to have been taxed at source, but at the 20% lower rate.

It is important to understand that income is divided between the various tax schedules, and to appreciate the tax treatment of the schedules relevant to you (most likely C to F).

Income under all schedules is added up when the Inland Revenue assesses your overall liability, taking into account personal allowances.

Personal allowances

The good news is that if you are a UK resident (but not necessarily if you are not a UK resident) you will not have to pay income tax on all your income. This is because every UK resident is granted a personal allowance which means that a certain amount of income in each tax year will not be subject to tax.

The table below lists the more common personal income tax allowances. You will find the figures printed in many magazines and tax tables, and usually in newspapers after the Chancellor of the Exchequer makes the annual budget statement (the Budget). The Chancellor usually changes the personal allowances each year by increasing them roughly in line with inflation. You need to keep up to date with changes to these amounts.

Income tax allowances for 1995/96	
Personal allowances	£3,525
Married couple's allowance	£1,720
Age allowance (age 65–74)	£4,630
Married couple's allowance (age 65–74)	£2,995
Age allowance (age 75 or over)	£4,800
Married couple's allowance (age 75 or over)	£3,035
Income limit for age allowance	£14,600
Additional personal relief for children (single parent)	£1,720
Widow's bereavement allowance	£1,720

Single person's allowance

If you are unmarried and under 65, in 1995/96 the first £3,525 you earn will not be taxed. This is called the personal allowance.

Married couple's allowance

If you are married, each spouse can earn up to £3,525 tax free. In addition, as a married couple you can earn a further £1,720 tax free. Since April 1993, at your choice, you can either have the married couple's allowance allocated to one of you, or it can be divided equally between both of you. Thus if in any particular tax year you or your spouse has not earned enough income to use the part of the married couple's allowance allocated, it can be transferred to the other spouse.

Relief on the married couple's allowance is 15% for 1995/96, so it is no longer a true deduction from income.

EXAMPLE

Suppose you are a married couple both aged 25. The man earns £4,000 a year, and the woman earns £15,000 a year.

	Man	**Woman**
Income	£4,000	£15,000
Less personal allowance	£3,525	£3,525
Subtotal	£475	£11,475

Now you can decide what to do with the married couple's allowance; in this case it would be sensible for the woman to claim the whole of the married couple's allowance, since the man's tax liability is very small (20% of £475 = £95).

IMPORTANT

If you do not use the whole of your allowance in any particular year, the difference canNOT be carried forward to another year – you have lost it forever. For this reason, it is important to get your claim right.

Age allowance

You will see from the table on page 80 that there are large allowances for people aged between 64 and 74, and even larger ones if you are aged 75 or over. In addition, the married couple's allowance for older people is increased. The married couple's allowance for those between 65 and 74 applies even if one partner is younger, and the same is true for those over 75.

EXAMPLE

Mr Smith is 54 and Mrs Smith is 67 in the tax year 1995/96. The allowances are initially as follows:

	Mr Smith	**Mrs Smith**
Personal allowances	£3,525	£4,630
Married couple's allowance	£2,995	

Supposing that Mr Smith earns less than £6,520, Mrs Smith could claim all or part of the married couple's allowance. If the tax saving is greater by allocating the married couple's allowance to Mrs Smith, she can claim half or all of the basic (but not age-related) married couple's allowance in any event.

Income limit for age allowance

In the table on page 80 you can see a figure for the income limit for the age allowance – this is £14,600 in 1995/96, and means that if you are claiming the age allowances, these increased allowances (i.e. the age allowances being higher than the ordinary allowances for those under the age of 65) are only available in full if you have an income of £14,600 or less.

If you are over 65 with an income in excess of this level, your allowance is reduced by £1 for every £2 by which the income exceeds £14,600.

EXAMPLE

Mr Brown is aged 76 and is single. His taxable income in 1995/96 is £15,200. What is his personal allowance?

Mr Brown will normally be entitled to the higher age allowance for a single person of £4,800, being over the age of 75. However, as his income exceeds the income limit for his age allowance by £600 (£15,200 less £14,600), his personal allowance will be reduced by half of this excess. The reduction to his personal allowance will be £300 (half of £600), making his revised figure for personal allowance £4,500 (£4,800 less £300).

If the rule had not existed, Mr Brown would have paid tax on all his income above his personal allowance of £4,800, which is £10,400 (£15,200–£4,800). With this rule he will now pay tax on all of his income above his revised personal allowance of £4,500, which is £10,700 (£15,200–£4,500).

Remember, though, that the age allowance can never be reduced below the ordinary allowance, however great the income. Thus, Mr Brown will always get a personal allowance of at least £3,525, however much his income increases.

The same principle applies to married couples, with the rule working to reduce the married couple's allowance, but only down to the standard rate of married couple's allowance, which is £1,720 in 1995/96.

Other allowances

There are a number of other personal allowances available in certain circumstances, the most common of which are:

- the additional personal allowance for children
- the widow's bereavement allowance

The additional personal allowance for children

This is claimed by single parents who are supporting children, in addition to their personal allowance. This effectively gives you the same total personal allowance as a married man. This extra allowance is a flat rate for a single parent regardless of the number of children they support.

The widow's bereavement allowance

This is an additional allowance granted, if you are a widow, in the tax year of your husband's death and in the following tax year. There is no similar allowance for husbands, although in the tax year of their wife's death they will still be granted the full married couple's allowance. This does not continue into the following year. Thus if the husband died in August 1993, his estate (assets) would still be granted the full offset against his taxable income before his date of death.

His wife would also, in that year, get a personal allowance and the widow's bereavement allowance (which is equivalent to the married couple's allowance), increasing her total personal allowance. This also applies in the following tax year, but after that the additional allowance will cease. If the widow also has dependent children, she can also claim the additional personal relief for children. Relief on both of these allowances is 20% for 1994/95 and 15% for 1995/96.

Income tax rates 1995/96

Taxable income (after deduction of allowances)		Rate	Total tax
First	£3,200	20%	£640
Next	£21,100	25%	£5,275
Over	£24,300	40%	

The lower rate of tax

> ### EXAMPLE
>
> Suppose you are a single woman aged 25 with an income of £4,525 in 1995/96. How much tax will you pay?
>
> - Your personal allowance is £3,525. £4,525–£3,525 = £1,000 taxable income.
> - The first £3,200 of taxable income is taxed at 20%. You have £1,000 of taxable income, so your tax will be £200.

The basic rate of tax

> ### EXAMPLE
>
> Suppose you are a single woman aged 25 with an income of £11,525 in 1995/96. How much tax will you pay?
>
> - Your personal allowance is £3,525. £11,525–£3,525 = £8,000 taxable income.
> - The first £3,200 of taxable income is taxed at 20% = £640.
> - The balance of your taxable income will be taxed at 25%; £8,000–£3,200 = £4,800. 25% of £4,800 is £1,200.
> - Adding the total tax together, we get:
>
> | | Tax |
> |---|---|
> | £3,200 taxed at 20% | £640 |
> | £4,800 taxed at 25% | £1,200 |
> | £8,000 total taxable income | £1,800 total tax |
>
> On your income of £11,525 you must pay £1,800 income tax.

The higher rate of tax

> ### EXAMPLE
>
> Many people do not earn enough to be liable for tax in the 40% band (which is over £27,825 in 1995/96 for a single person including the personal allowance). Let's suppose, though, that you are a single woman earning £32,525 in 1995/96. How much tax would you pay?

- Your personal allowance is £3,525. £32,525–£3,525 = £29,000 taxable income.
- The first £3,200 of taxable income is taxed at 20% = £640.
- The next £21,100 of your taxable income will be taxed at 25% = £5,275.
- The balance of your taxable income will be taxed at 40%; this balance is £29,000–(£3,200+£21,100) = £4,700. 40% of £4,700 is £1,880.
- Adding the total tax together, we get:

	Tax
£3,200 taxed at 20%	£640
£21,100 taxed at 25%	£5,275
£4,700 taxed at 40%	£1,880
£29,000 total taxable income	£7,795 total tax

On your income of £32,525 you must pay £7,795 income tax.

Summary

These bands of income tax rates, also known as marginal rates, are a relatively new invention and are liable to change in the future. For this reason, it is important to stay alert and keep yourself informed about current changes. A bonus, a pay rise, or an unexpectedly successful investment can all push you into a new band, and, unless you plan for it, you could find yourself paying more income tax than you expected – get help from an accountant.

Benefits in kind

Many companies offer benefits in addition to salary to selected employees. The most common of these are:

- a company car (most often for sales reps)
- cheaper mortgages and loans (most commonly to employees of banks and building societies).

These benefits can be a mixed blessing, particularly in the case of loans, since employers can psychologically tie you to them with this method (i.e. if you leave, you may have to borrow elsewhere at a higher rate to repay the employer). However, here we are examining the tax implications; the Inland Revenue treats these benefits as if they are earned income, even though you do not actually receive the money.

- Employees earning less than 38,500 will often be exempt from this rule and may enjoy such benefits without liability to income tax.
- Benefits in kind rules are not applied to the self-employed, who are taxed differently.

EXAMPLE

Suppose you are a single man aged 28 with an income of £35,000, and have borrowed £10,000 from your firm at a low rate of interest. Suppose also that the difference between this low rate of interest and rates at which you could have borrowed elsewhere is 5%. The benefit in kind would therefore be 5% of £10,000 = £500. this would reduce your personal allowance from £3,525 to £3,025. Taking this into account, your tax would be:

No tax on	£3,025	
20% tax on	£3,200	£640
25% tax on	£21,100	£5,275
40% tax on	£7,675	£3,070
Total income:	£35,000	Total tax: £8,985

—— Filling in income tax returns ——

If you have taxable income or investments, you or your accountant will probably have to complete a tax return each year. For employed people, the return will be sent to you for the previous tax year (April 6th of one year to April 5th of the next). Normally you will have to complete the form and return it to your tax office within 30 days of receiving it. There are a few general rules about filling in your return.

- Make sure you give full and accurate information.
- Double check your return to make sure you have left nothing out.
- Always keep a copy of your return.

If you simply earn a wage and have no financial commitments or claimable expenses, filling in the return is fairly straightforward. You will need your P60 form for the relevant year (which your employer will give you) in order to complete the earnings section. You will also need to indicate if you are entitled to claim for such allowances as the married couple's allowance, widow's allowance and single parent's allowance. The tax return comes with a leaflet which explains each section of the form, but if you have any queries you can telephone your tax office, and they will explain. However, the more complex your financial affairs are, the more difficult it is to complete the tax return. The return is divided into the following sections.

Earnings

This asks for information on wages, tips, employment expenses, benefits in kind (non-cash benefits), profit-sharing schemes, income from self-employment and various trade union and friendly society assurance policies.

Pensions and benefits

This asks for details on pensions, unemployment benefit and income support that you have received in the relevant tax year.

Pensions you expect to receive in the following year

Other income

This includes income from National Savings, bank and building society accounts, unit trust income, share dividends, income from property, maintenance and alimony income and income from trusts.

Legally binding maintenance or alimony payments

This asks for the amount you were ordered by a court to pay and the amount you have actually paid.

Mortgage or loan for main home

This asks for details of your mortgage.

Other deductions

This includes charitable donations and other loans which qualify for tax relief.

Payments you have made abroad

Capital gains you have made during the year

Your tax allowances

This includes boxes to tick if you are entitled to tax allowances other than the basic personal allowance, which is deducted automatically.

Personal details

This asks for your address and National Insurance number if they have changed, and your marital status.

Declaration

You must sign the form here, stating that the information you have given is 'correct and complete to the best of your knowledge and belief'.

The Inland Revenue will then use the tax return to calculate if you have any more tax to pay, or if you are entitled to a refund. If you think they have made a mistake, you can challenge the assessment.

Unless your financial situation is very straightforward, or you understand the tax rules very well, you would be well advised to pay a professional adviser, preferably a charted accountant, to help you fill in your return. They will charge a fee, and it is worth shopping around to find one that is reasonable. While this may seem an unnecessary expense, a good accountant will save you a lot of trouble and may also be able to save you some tax as well, by his or her superior knowledge of the rules.

Self-assessment

The tax return system is currently being changed to a 'self-assessment' system, which is supposed to be simpler. The first self-assessment returns will be sent out in April 1997; you will be required to fill in the figures yourself, and then either:

- work out your own tax assessment and return the form by January 31st 1998, or
- return the form by the end of September 1997 and let the Inland Revenue work out your assessment.

The major difference with self-assessment is that taxpayers will be required to keep more records than they did before. From April 1996 you should start keeping such records as:

- P60, P160, P11D, P9D and P2K and P45 forms

- Payslips and pay statements
- Notes of tips and gratuities
- Certificates for 'Taxed Award' schemes
- Pension certificates and statements
- Any details you have received from the Benefits Agency and the Employment Services Agency relating to state benefits and pensions
- Bank and building society statements, chequebooks and passbooks
- Interest statements from other investments
- Tax deduction certificates from your bank
- Vouchers and statements relating to unit trusts you own
- All information on shares you buy, own or sell
- Life insurance chargeable event certificates
- Details of income you receive from a trust

In short, you must keep full records relating to any financial transactions or commitments. The Inland Revenue says that you only have to keep these records for 22 months after the end of the relevant tax year, but it makes sense to keep your records for much longer than this, particularly if your affairs are complex.

Self-employed people are already required to keep such records, but the self-assessment system is on a 'current year basis', so instead of paying tax on profits made in the year before the year of the tax return, you will pay tax on the profits arising in the tax year itself. 1996/97 will be a 'catch-up' year where an average of your profits will be taxed. You should discuss how to handle this with your accountant.

——— National Insurance (NI) ———

You may wonder why National Insurance contributions are included in the tax chapter. These payments are not officially called a tax, and the rates are proposed to Parliament by the Secretary of State for Social Security, rather than the Chancellor of the Exchequer. In reality, however, National Insurance contributions are indeed a tax; they must be paid by the employed and the self-employed (where earnings exceed a certain level) and by employers. Almost all National Insurance contributions are collected with income tax and then paid by the Inland Revenue to the Department of Social Security. The DSS receives some contributions direct.

A small proportion of the total contributions received by the DSS is passed to the National Health Service Account and the rest is paid to the National Insurance Fund. The major state social security benefits such as retirement pensions, widow's benefit, unemployment and invalidity benefits are paid from the National Insurance Fund.

Despite its name, National Insurance is not insurance at all – the money you contribute is not invested for you, but is paid out directly to others; there is no real guarantee that, if you are young now, you will receive benefits in old age because of your contributions during your working life. This is an area of significant concern at the moment because the UK, like most other rich countries, has as 'ageing population', which means that people are living longer than they used to, and relatively few children are being born; this trend, which is likely to continue, may result in massive numbers of pensioners being supported by a small number of working people in the next century. How this is going to be handled is anybody's guess, but the present system will inevitably be adjusted, and some people may suffer. National Insurance contributions are in practice a kind of taxation on the income of employees, the self-employed and employers.

As we will see in Chapter 8, the social security system has a large number of benefits which you can claim in various circumstances. An important point is that if you do not fulfil the required level of contributions (which varies) of the appropriate NI class to qualify for certain benefits, you will not be able to claim these benefits even if you are otherwise eligible.

The classes of National Insurance

The classes, or categories, of National Insurance are levied on different kinds of income, but never on investment income or pension schemes. The classes are as follows.

Class 1

This relates to employees. It is divided into primary Class 1 NI, which is paid by you the employee, and secondary Class 1 NI, which is paid by your employer. The rate of contribution is a percentage of what you earn.

Class 2

This is a flat-rate NI payment paid by the self-employed, unless you have very low profits.

Class 3

These are voluntary contributions which may be paid if you want to maintain or improve your rights to certain state benefits.

Class 4

This class is also payable by the self-employed as a percentage of all profits between a lower and an upper limit.

Class 1 National Insurance

This is paid by all employees who have salaries more than a 'lower earnings level' (LEL), which in 1995/96 is £59 per week or £3,068 per year. The level increases each year in line with inflation. Paying this class of National Insurance qualifies you for state benefits, in particular:

- sickness benefits
- basic old age pension and, possibly, SERPS.

Employees contracted-in to SERPS

If you are contracted-in to SERPS you should note from the table on page 94 that employees with earnings more than the lower earnings limit pay National Insurance at 2% of the first £59 per week of their earnings and 10% of their earnings more than this. There is also an 'upper earnings level' – no-one pays NI on earnings they have over £440 a week or £22,880 a year (1995/96 figures).

EXAMPLE FOR LOWER EARNERS

Suppose you are employed and contracted-in to SERPS, and you earn £6,000 a year. How much Class 1 National Insurance will you pay in the 1995/96 tax year?

2% of the first	£3,068	£61.36
10% of	£2,932	£293.20
Total earned income £6,000	Total Class 1 contributions	£354.56

EXAMPLE FOR HIGHER EARNERS

Suppose you are employed and contracted-in to SERPS, and you earn £30,000 a year. How much Class 1 National Insurance will you pay in the 1995/96 tax year?

2% of the first	£3,068	£61.36
10% of the balance (up to the upper earnings limit)	£19,812	£1,981.20
0% on £7,120 (over the upper earnings limit)		–
Total earned income£30,000	Total Class 1 contributions £2,042.56	

Employees who are contracted-out of SERPS

If you are an employee who has decided to contract-out of SERPS by using an appropriate personal pension (APP), then the amount of Class 1 contributions you pay will be exactly the same; the Department of Social Security (DSS) calculates the amount of your rebate annually and sends that amount to the APP provider (usually an insurance company) which you have chosen.

If you are an employee who has contracted-out of SERPS because of a decision by your employer, through an occupational pension scheme, you can see from the table on page 94 that you will pay a reduced level of National Insurance on your earnings between the lower and upper earnings limits; this is known as your middle earnings band (MEB).

This reduction is currently at 1.8%, which makes the normal Class 1 rate of NI 8.2%. Note that earnings below £59 per week at still liable to NI at 2% unless your total earnings are below £59 per week, in which case you will pay no National Insurance, and earnings over the upper earnings limit are not liable to further National Insurance.

How Class 1 contributions are collected

Primary Class 1 contributions (the ones that you, the employee, make) are collected by your employer and paid monthly to the local collector of taxes together with the secondary Class 1 contributions (the ones that your employer makes on your behalf). The Inland Revenue then pays this to the DSS.

Class 2 and Class 4 National Insurance

These are paid by people who are self-employed. Class 2 National Insurance is a flat rate weekly payment, £5.85 in 1995/96, which must be paid by all self-employed people who earn more than £3,310 in 1995/96. Class 4 National Insurance is paid on profits over £6,640 in 1995/96; it is 7.3% of your profits between the lower limit of £6,640 and an upper limit of £22,880 in 1995/96. Half of any Class 4 contributions you make are allowable against your income tax.

EXAMPLE FOR LOWER EARNERS

Suppose you are self-employed and earning £4,000 in profits in 1995/96.

Class 2 contributions are £5.85 per week. This is all you will pay.

EXAMPLE FOR HIGHER EARNERS

Suppose you are self-employed and earning £12,000 in profits in 1995/96. How much National Insurance contribution must you make?

Class 2 contributions are £5.85 per week.

To calculate Class 4 contributions subtract the lower Class 4 limit from your profits:

£12,000–£6,640 = £5,360

7.3% of £5,360 is £391.28

You will pay £5.85 per week Class 2 contributions and £391.28 for the year's Class 4 contributions.

EXAMPLE FOR EVEN HIGHER EARNERS

Suppose you are self-employed and earning £42,000 in profits in 1995/96. How much National Insurance contribution must you make?

Class 2 contributions are £5.85 per week. To calculate Class 4 contributions subtract the lower Class 4 limit from the upper Class 4 limit:

£22,880–£6,640 = £16,240

7.3% of £16,240 is £1,185.52.

You will pay £5.85 per week Class 2 contributions and £1,185.52 for the year's Class 4 contributions.

Class 3 National Insurance

Class 3 contributions can be made by anyone who is not paying either Class 1 or Class 2 contributions because their income is below the level at which you pay those classes. It is a flat rate of £5.75 per week.

YOUR CONTRIBUTIONS AS AN EMPLOYEE		
Earnings	**Contracted-in**	**Contracted-out**
£59–£440 per week	2% on first £59 plus 10% on earnings between £59 and £440	2% on first £59 plus 8.2% on earnings between £59 and £440
Some widows and married women may pay a lower rate		
Class 2 (Self-employed)		
Earnings over £3,310 per annum	£5.85 a week from April 1995	
Class 3 (voluntary)	£5.75 per week	
Class 4 (Self-employed, additional levy)		
Profits between £6,640 and £22,880 per annum	7.3%	

8
——— BENEFITS ———

Social security benefits are paid by the Government, usually through the Department of Social Security (DSS). There is a very wide range available, but generally you are eligible for them because of:

- your age
- the state of your health
- your level of income or employment status
- the fact that you are caring for children.

One of the peculiarities of the system is that your entitlement to any particular social security benefit may be affected if you are also receiving other social security benefits.

The changing social security system

As everyone knows, the social security system has been the subject of furious political debate for decades; whatever your personal feelings on the subject, however, it is important to realise that social security systems are undergoing fundamental changes all across Europe. Governments frequently tinker with the details of the benefits rules for all kinds of reasons, but there is an overall problem; the richer European countries (including the UK) have ageing populations, which means that, in general, people are living much longer than they used to, and need to be cared for more. This means that the cost of the social security system is growing dramatically. A practical implication is that you cannot rely on the benefit system to work in the future in the way it has up to now. This is particularly important when planning for your old age. To give an example of benefit cuts, consider SERPS (State Earnings Related Pension Scheme, see page 152), which has been reduced in value over the last few years.

National Insurance

Many benefits are based on your National Insurance contributions; the National Insurance system is changing, and is becoming more and more of a tax, rather than an 'insurance', which it was originally intended to be. See Chapter 7, Tax and National Insurance (page 71) for details of the system.

Survival strategies

The social security system is going through a period of transition, and no-one can be perfectly sure what the outcome will be. In the meantime, it is very easy to get upset and confused by the complexity of the system, which is heavily bureaucratic. If you need to claim benefit and have not had much experience in doing so, here are a few dos and don'ts:

Do realise that in many cases the DSS officers have some discretionary powers; try to find out what these are in your case.

Do realise that most benefits are not currently designed to make life comfortable; they provide barely enough to get by on.

Don't make benefit claiming into a career if you want to be a good money manager.

Don't be surprised if the rules seem to keep changing while you are claiming.

What is the range of benefits?

The full list of all benefits is very complex and liable to change; it would take the whole of this book even to explain the main benefits completely. In this chapter we will concentrate on the main ones. If you want to know more, get leaflet LB2, 'Which Benefit?' from your local Department of Social Security (DSS) office or from a post office, which gives a general overview of benefits and contributions. Most social security benefits are paid if you are in one of these situations.

- You are unemployed or on low income
- You are bringing up children
- You are retired
- You are sick or disabled

Currently, different benefits have different tax, means and contribution rules applied to them; the details of these rules are likely to change in the future. Benefits may or may not be:

- taxable as earned income
- dependent upon a certain number of National Insurance contributions
- free from tax
- means tested on income and/or capital (savings).

'Means testing' means that you have to have less than a certain amount of income or savings in order to be eligible for a particular benefit.

Benefits if you are unemployed or on a low income

In this section we will look at:

- Redundancy payments
- Family credit
- Unemployment benefit
- Income support
- Some other social security benefits

Statutory redundancy payments

Purpose

Redundancy payments are designed to give compensation to you if you lose your job because of redundancy. They are paid by the employer by law in a lump sum and are tax free.

Features

The payment is made without means testing, and without regard to your future job prospects. Even if you are a millionaire and are about to walk into another job, you are still entitled to statutory redundancy pay. While statutory redundancy payments are not liable to tax, many employers give more than the statutory minimum, and this extra, if it is more than £30,000, is taxable. Note that:

- You are not eligible if you have worked for your employer for less than two years.

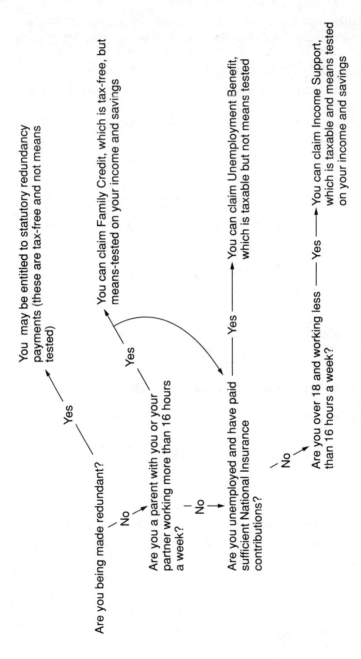

Fig 8.1

- Your eligibility is not affected by receiving other social security benefits.

How the payment is calculated

The amount is based on the number of the years you have worked and your age at the time of redundancy. The maximum statutory redundancy payment is just over £6,000 pounds and the maximum number of years which can be taken into account is 20. You are granted a maximum amount of one and a half week's pay for each year of service, depending on your age, and the maximum level of pay which can be taken into account in the calculation is currently a little over £200 a week.

Family credit

Purpose

This is a tax-free benefit for families with children where at least one of the parents is working at least 16 hours per week. The maximum weekly rate is £45.15 in 1995/96 for each adult, with lower weekly rates for each child.

Features

- You are eligible whether you are self-employed or employed.
- Although 'family credit' sounds as if it is some kind of loan, it is not a loan and does not have to be repaid.
- It does not matter whether or not you have previously paid National Insurance contributions, but family credit is means tested. How much you receive depends on your family's total income including some social security benefits.
- The level of family credit you receive also depends on any savings you have. If you have savings of more than £3,000, you will receive less benefit, and if you have savings of more than £8,000 you will not be eligible.
- For families who receive family credit, certain other social security benefits also become payable. These include housing benefit, which gives a weekly allowance towards housing costs, such as rent, with the maximum level of benefit dependent on the number of people in the family.
- Housing benefit and other benefits such as one parent benefit, child benefit and attendance allowance (see pages 101 – 110) are not

taken into consideration when calculating the amount of family credit but most other major kinds of benefit are, and will reduce the level of family credit.

Unemployment benefit

Purpose

Unemployment benefit is taxable, and is only payable to people who have qualified by paying sufficient Class 1 National Insurance contributions (see page 90) while they were working. If you do not meet the National Insurance contribution requirements, you must try to obtain other benefits instead, in particular income support. If you are eligible for unemployment benefit, you may also be able to claim some income support depending on your circumstances (see below).

The weekly level of unemployment benefit is £46.45 for someone under pension age and £59.15 for someone over pension age (65 for men and 60 for women).

Features

- You must be able to show that you are actively seeking employment, which means that you must be fit for work (healthy) and available for work.
- Unemployment benefit is a flat rate, with an additional amount payable if you are supporting another adult.
- It is not means tested and is not dependent on your level of savings.
- The rules mean that it is unlikely that you will be receiving any other benefits, but where these are being paid, very few affect the level of unemployment benefit you can claim.

Income support

Purpose

Anyone over the age of 18 who works less than 16 hours per week (and is thus unable to claim family credit) may be able to claim income support, which is taxable and means tested. You must show that you are 'taking reasonable steps' to find a job. Income support is not dependent on having paid National Insurance contributions.

Features

- Any savings you have over £3,000 will reduce the level of benefit you receive.
- The actual amount of income support you receive depends on several factors, perhaps the most important of which is the level of income coming into the household (including any social security benefits) and whether you are supporting others.
- The amount of income support can be amended to help meet the cost of mortgage interest and some other housing costs not met by housing benefit.
- You may also be able to get help with the cost of NHS treatment, rent and other outgoings.

Other social security benefits

If you are on a low income (whether you are employed or self-employed), you may be able to claim some other social security benefits, including:

- help with certain NHS costs such as prescriptions and dental treatment
- help with the cost of housing (rent and mortgage interest).

Benefits if you are bringing up children

In this section we will look at:

- Child benefit
- Statutory maternity pay
- Benefits for one-parent families
- Family credit

Child benefit

Purpose

This is the main benefit for people who are looking after a child under the age of 16, or up to 18 if the child is in full-time education. It does not matter if you are a 'birth parent', an adoptive parent or a foster parent. It is tax free and is not means tested. At present (from April

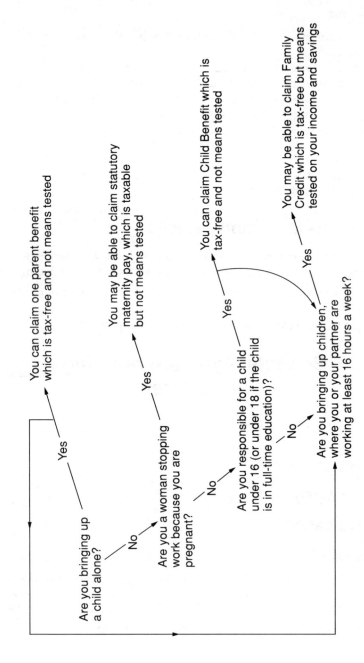

Fig 8.2 Bringing up children

1995) the child benefit payment for the first child is £10.40 a week, and for each subsequent child you receive £8.45 a week.

Features

- Child benefit can begin as soon as the child is born, and is payable as a flat-rate weekly amount for each child.
- This benefit is not dependent upon your National Insurance contributions.
- If you have not claimed this benefit when you first became eligible, it can be backdated for up to 12 months.
- The entitlement to child benefit is not affected by any other benefits received by the claimant.

Statutory maternity pay

Purpose

Statutory maternity pay is paid by your employer to you if you stop work because you are pregnant. The benefit is taxable and it is also liable for Class 1 National Insurance contributions, just as earned income is. It is not means tested.

Features

- You are only eligible if you have previously worked for your employer for at least six months and are earning enough to pay Class 1 National Insurance contributions (see page 90).
- If the rules on continuous employment and earnings are met, then for the first six weeks of absence the payment is at 90% of the level of your previous average earnings.
- After six weeks the amount falls to the lower level of £52.50 per week for the next 12 weeks and then finishes altogether.
- If you are not entitled to statutory maternity pay, but have recently been employed or self-employed (and have paid either Class 1 or Class 2 National Insurance contributions), you may be eligible for a different DSS benefit called maternity allowance.
- Maternity allowance is at a lower rate than statutory maternity pay. It is £45.55 a week in 1995/96 for a maximum of 18 weeks. It is tax free and there is no liability to National Insurance contributions.
- Entitlement to maternity allowance is affected if you are receiving unemployment or sickness benefit, but most other kinds of social security benefit will not affect your entitlement.

Benefits for one-parent families

Purpose

If you are bringing up a child on your own, you are entitled to one-parent benefit, whether you are separated, divorced or widowed. It is a flat-rate payment for one child only of £6.30 per week from April 1995, and is tax free. It is not means tested, and does not depend on previous payment of National Insurance contributions.

Features

- Single-parent family benefit is usually unaffected by receipt of most other social security benefits.

- Remember that there is an additional income tax allowance for one-parent families (see page 80). The extra allowance, currently equal to the married couple's allowance (see page 80), is added to the single person's allowance.

- If you are a widow with children you are supporting, you may also be eligible for a further benefit if your late husband had paid sufficient National Insurance contributions. This is called the widowed mother's allowance, and is payable in addition to child benefit. For 1995/96, this allowance is £59.15 per week, and is taxable.

Family credit

Purpose

This benefit is designed for working families on low incomes who are supporting children. See page 99 for details.

Financial planning when you have a family and are receiving social security benefits

Most working families would probably see the social security benefits that they might be entitled to as being too low for the standard of living they would like. For this reason, many families take out insurance so that if their earned income drops they will still be able to keep up their standard of living. See Chapter 9.

Some families don't actually need the child benefit payment to make ends meet; if you are in this position, think about using this money (which is a regular sum) to put into a savings plan of some kind, or using it for insurance.

Benefits if you are sick or disabled

In this section we will look at:

- Statutory sick pay
- Invalidity benefit
- Sickness benefit
- Severe disablement allowance
- Other benefits for the disabled

Statutory sick pay (SSP)

Purpose

If you work for an employer (*not* if you are self-employed) and earn enough to pay Class 1 National Insurance contributions, you will usually be entitled to statutory sick pay (SSP) if you are unable to work due to sickness for more than three days in a row. For 1995/96, the rate of SSP is £52.50 per week.

Features

- SSP is paid by the employer (who then reclaims it from the DSS) for up to 28 weeks in each period of sickness, after which invalidity benefit becomes payable.
- The benefit is taxable as earned income and you, the employee, must also pay Class 1 National Insurance contributions on the payments just as if they were earnings.
- SSP is not means tested.

Invalidity benefit

Invalidity benefit is designed to help you if you are off work for more than 28 weeks because you are sick. It is in two parts.

- Invalidity pension
- Invalidity allowance

In 1995/96, invalidity pension is £59.15 per week; the maximum level of invalidity allowance is £12.40 per week.

Features

- Invalidity pension is a flat-rate pension which increases if you are supporting others, and may also be increased by an earnings-related additional pension (i.e. benefits from SERPS, see page 152).

- The invalidity allowance is a further flat-rate addition to the pension, and is payable if you become sick more than five years before your retirement age.

- In order to be eligible, you must have:
  (a) been incapable for work for 28 weeks
  (b) previously received either SSP, sickness benefit (which both finish after 28 weeks), or statutory maternity pay, and
  (c) been incapable of work due to illness or disablement.

- You must also have paid a certain required level of National Insurance contributions. If you have not done so, you may be able to claim severe disablement allowance instead.
- Invalidity benefit is not means tested and is tax free.
- It continues until you return to work or retire.

Sickness benefit

Purpose

If you are off work because of sickness for more than three consecutive days, and are not able to claim SSP – for example, if you are self-employed – you may be able to claim sickness benefit. It is payable for up to 28 weeks, after which you may be able to claim invalidity benefit.

Sickness benefit is not means tested or taxable but does depend on your having paid enough National Insurance contributions, unless you are ill because of an accident at work or an industrial disease, in which case this condition may be waived. The weekly rates in 1995/96 are £56.75 for someone over pensionable (60 for women, 65 for men) and £44.40 per week for someone under pensionable age.

BENEFITS FOR THE SICK AND DISABLED

If you are:	Benefit	Taxable?	Means tested?
Employed, paying Class 1 National Insurance contributions, and become sick for more than three consecutive days	Statutory sick pay	Taxable	No
Off work due to sickness for more than 28 weeks, and have previously received statutory sick pay, sickness benefit or statutory maternity pay	Invalidity benefit	Tax free	No
Off work due to sickness for more than three consecutive days and are ineligible for statutory sick pay	Sickness benefit	Tax free	No
Off work for more than 28 weeks due to illness but cannot receive invalidity pension due to insufficient National Insurance contributions	Severe disablement allowance	Tax free	No

Fig 8.3

Features

- The level of sickness benefit is lower than that of SSP.
- There are enhanced rates and additional sickness benefit if you are supporting another adult.

Severe disablement allowance

If you have been unable to work for at least 28 weeks due to illness, but cannot receive invalidity pension because you have not paid sufficient National Insurance contributions, you may be able to claim severe disablement allowance. The basic weekly rate for 1995/96 is £35.90, with age-related additions ranging up to £12.40.

Features

- Severe disablement allowance is a flat-rate benefit with age-related additions and increases if you are supporting a spouse and/or children.
- If your illness or disability began after reaching state pension age, you are not eligible.
- The allowance is not means tested and is paid free of tax.

Other benefits for the disabled

There are many other social security benefits available for people who are physically or mentally disabled.

Disability living allowance (DLA)

This is a tax-free benefit for people under 65 who need help with personal care, getting around or both. It combines a care component payable at one of the three weekly rates of £12.40, £31.20 or £46.55 and a mobility component (for those over five years old) paid at one of two rates, £12.40 or £32.65, depending on how much help is required.

Disability working allowance

This may be available for people aged 16 or over who are working at least 16 hours a week but whose illness or disability limits their earning capacity. It is a tax-free income-related benefit, available in addition to any DLA payments.

OTHER BENEFITS FOR THE DISABLED

If you are:	Benefit	Taxable?	Means tested?
Under 65 and need help in getting around and/or personal care	Disability living allowance	Tax free	No
Over 16 and working at least 16 hours a week but have your earning capacity limited by sickness or disability	Disability working allowance	Tax free	Related to your income
Over 65 and need care because of a severe mental or physical handicap which began after the age of 65	Attendance allowance	Tax free	No
Of working age and spend a lot of time looking after someone who is disabled and receiving DLA or attendance allowance	Invalid care allowance	Taxable	No

Fig 8.4

Attendance allowance

This is a weekly cash benefit for those who need a lot of looking after because of a severe physical or mental handicap and whose illness or disability began after the age of 65. It is equivalent to the care benefits available under DLA for those under 65. It is tax free.

Invalid care allowance

This is a weekly cash benefit, but it is taxable. It is for people of working age who spend a lot of time looking after and caring for someone severely disabled who receives DLA or an attendance allowance.

All benefits are usually paid in addition to the other sickness benefits outlined above.

Social security benefits for pensioners

Apart from the other social security benefits you can claim if you are on a low income, the main state benefits if you are retired are:

- the basic state pension
- the State Earnings-Related Pension Scheme (SERPS).

The basic state pension

Purpose

Almost everyone in the UK can claim this when they reach the age of 60 for women or 65 for men. The weekly level in 1995/96 is £59.15, with an additional £35.30 for a wife claiming the pension on the basis of her husband's contribution record.

Features

- Whether or not you will receive the full amount of the basic state pension depends on your National Insurance contribution record.
- Your entitlement to this pension can be gained in one of three main ways:
  - (a) The most common way is from the payment of National Insurance contributions, either Class 1 (for employees), Class 2

BENEFITS FOR PENSIONER

If you are:	Benefit	Taxable?	Means tested?
Over 65 and a man, or over 60 and a woman	Basic state pension	Taxable	No
Over 65 and a man, or over 60 and a woman, and have been an employee paying Class 1 National Insurance contributions and have not been contracted out of SERPS	State Earnings Related Pension Scheme (SERPS)	Taxable	No

Fig 8.5

(for the self-employed) or Class 3 (voluntary contributions from people who want to build up their entitlement but do not pay either Class 1 or Class 2 contributions).

(b) You may be able to get contribution credits if you have been receiving unemployment benefit, sickness benefit, invalidity pension, severe disablement allowance or payments for approved training. If so, you will be treated as if you actually had paid sufficient National Insurance contributions.

(c) A married woman may be able to claim a reduced level of basic state pension on the basis of National Insurance contributions paid by her husband.

- The benefit is taxable; it is not means tested and it is not affected if you are receiving other social security benefits.

State Earnings-Related Pension Scheme (SERPS)

Purpose

If you have been an employee (but not if you have been self-employed), you may be entitled to benefits from SERPS. SERPS is a 'top up' state pension scheme into which employees who are liable to Class 1 National Insurance make contributions and receive taxable benefits from the state pension age.

In total the benefits from SERPS cannot exceed 25% of your 'middle band' earnings (see page 85). This limit reduces to 20% for employees retiring after the year 2000.

SERPS are explained in more detail in Chapter 10. Pensions (page 144).

Features

- The contributions you make while you are employed are part of the normal (full) Class 1 contribution rates and are not separately payable nor separately identified.
- It is possible for an employer's occupational pension scheme to contract out its members from SERPS, which would mean that if you were a member you would not be due to benefit from SERPS (although any benefits you had accumulated before being contracted-out, with your current or any previous employer, would be safe).

- You may contract out of SERPS yourself through an 'appropriate personal pension' (APP) (see page 156).

—— Other social security benefits ——

As well as the major benefits we have looked at so far in this chapter, there is a wide range of other benefits. These include:

A means tested grant from the DSS social fund to help with funeral expenses
Help with NHS charges
Student grants and loans
The widow's payment, which is a tax-free lump sum paid to a widow on the death of her husband.

The widow's payment

Currently this is £1,000. Every widow will qualify for this unless she and her husband were over pensionable age and he was receiving a state pension when he died. It depends on the National Insurance contribution record of the husband, but there is a very low level of required contributions, so the vast majority of 'young' widows will qualify.

—————— Conclusion ——————

In the vast majority of cases, social security benefits are not enough to help people keep up the standard of living they enjoyed when they had a full level of earned income, nor, if you have never had such income, will they provide more than the bare necessities (you may not feel they even provide that). Whatever the rights and wrongs of the system are, and they are always the subject of furious political debate, these are the painful facts, and, as discussed at the beginning of the chapter, state benefits are not likely to become much more generous in the future, whatever political party is in power. If, like many people, you want to attain financial prosperity, there are several things you can do.

- Increase your income through employment or self-employment (see Chapter 5).

- Train yourself to become a good money manager.
- Get the savings habit (see Chapter 5).
- Learn about investment. This complex subject is touched upon in Chapter 5; it is too vast to be treated properly in this book, but there are many good introductory books available (see the Bibliography). Remember that the art and science of investment is something which you get better and better at the more you practise it.

You don't have to be a genius or highly talented to achieve prosperity, and it is never too late to start.

And remember, state benefits are a god-send if you are in trouble and can't get help elsewhere, so it is important to take them into account when you are planning.

9
—— INSURANCE ——

'Insurance', 'assurance', 'whole life' – there's almost a dictionary's worth of insurance jargon carrying associations with over-eager sales-people and faceless, soulless institutions. Nevertheless, we all need to learn something about insurance, which everyone needs at one time or another.

In this chapter we will look at:

- House (building and contents) insurance
- Car insurance
- Travel insurance
- Claiming on an insurance policy
- Protection products
- Basic life assurance – 'term assurance'
- 'Whole of life' insurance
- Health insurance
- General protection insurance
- Surrender values
- Choosing an insurance policy

Common misunderstandings about insurance

The main theme of all selling of insurance is fear. What if you died tomorrow? What if the house burned down? What if you had a heart attack? These are all important questions which we should consider, but not necessarily in the company of a salesperson; the point is that the benefit offered (money in case of a disaster) may or may not be worth the premiums you must pay. It really is worth getting independent advice on insurance (see page 38), because it is all too easy to end up with the wrong kind of policy.

When you buy insurance, you should always check the terms of the policy carefully. Make sure that you understand the exclusions; for example, your insurance could be invalid if you go parachuting, even if your claim has nothing to do with parachuting. It is not possible to insure against everything, and if you tried you would spend all your money on buying insurance.

Insurance works on probability, which is a mathematical discipline. When an insurance company sells you a policy, it is taking a gamble that either you will not make a claim, or, with some types of insurance, the amount you will claim will be less than the amount you pay in premiums.

Insurance companies use expert statisticians, called actuaries, to calculate the overall chances of individuals in a particular category making claims; they then set the price of the insurance premiums to cover what they expect to pay out in claims overall. This makes it worthwhile to insure yourself against certain risks, where the loss you would sustain if you as an individual suffered a disaster is much higher than the premiums you must pay. For example, taking out travel insurance, and insuring against your house burning down, are both cases where your loss, if you had one, would be much higher than the cost of the premiums. If you wanted to insure valuable antiques, however, you might find that the premiums were so high that it wasn't worth it.

The risks that you can insure against, and the cost of the insurance, can vary dramatically over time. For example, redundancy insurance (see page 140) has become harder to obtain as the chances of being made redundant have increased. If in the future there was full employment in the UK, the cost of redundancy insurance would probably come down.

Basic insurance

There are many everyday insurances that you will take out at one time or another. How much insurance cover you should buy depends ultimately on your attitude towards the potential loss – if you drive an old banger, for example, are you sure you need to pay for expensive fully comprehensive cover? Insurance companies make money out of the premiums you pay, so make sure you aren't paying a fortune for insurance when you could be putting the money into your savings instead.

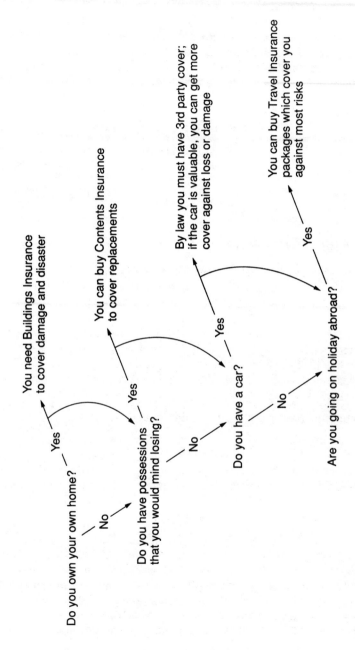

Fig 9.1 Everyday insurance

Excess figures

Many policies require you to pay a fixed part of any claim – say, the first £50 or first £500. This makes the insurance premiums cheaper to you and, in general, a policy with an excess is a better bargain than one without.

House and contents insurance

Insuring your home comes in two parts – the building itself, and the contents.

Building insurance

If you own your own house, you will probably have this insurance, which protects you against damage to the building. If you live in rented accommodation you do not need this insurance. Check that the amount insured for re-building your home is sufficient, and that the details of your house are accurate. You should also check that you are insured against other people being injured on your premises (third party liability). If you buy this insurance through a mortgage lender, you may be paying over the odds, so make sure you shop around for the best deal.

Buildings insurance is a fairly standard product. It covers:

- Your building
- The roof
- The windows
- Internal and external fixtures (including such things as cupboards and electrical wiring)
- Garages, outhouses and patios (usually)

(Items such as fences and swimming pools are not usually fully covered.)

The insurance usually protects you against damage from the weather, theft, riots, vandalism, traffic accidents, legal costs and compensation expenses if someone sues you for damages caused by your property, for example if your roof tiles fall and damage another person's property. Normally the property is not covered if you leave it unoccupied for more than 30 days; if you are going to leave the house empty for some time, you should contact the insurer for extra cover.

The main problem with buildings insurance is deciding how much to insure for. You have to buy enough insurance to cover the maximum amount the insurer might have to pay out – so it should cover, for example, the full cost of rebuilding your house if it were burned to the ground. If you don't insure to that level, any claim you make will be subject to 'averaging', which means that if, say, you have only insured to half the value, all payouts on claims will be cut in half.

To check the rebuilding value, get an up-to-date guide from your insurer or broker which gives detailed tables for the exact size of your locality of your house; you can use this to work out the insurance value. Some insurers do not require you to do this, but simply quote you a premium depending on the type of building and location and covering you for the worst case scenario – this saves a lot of measuring and arithmetic.

Contents insurance

Contents insurance covers damage or loss of your possessions. Most policies will pay out enough on claims to buy brand new articles to replace those you have lost; to get this cover you will often have to make a detailed estimate of the replacement value of all your possessions. Here is an example of a checklist you could use to work this out.

Contents checklist

Replacement value

High risk articles
Jewellery
Pictures and works of art
TVs, computers, video and
audio equipment
Clocks, cameras, binoculars
Furs

Other articles
Dining room
Sofa/suite
Chairs

Fire
Carpet
Curtains
Cutlery
Glass
Other
Kitchen
Refrigerator
Freezer & contents
Cooker
Washing machine/dryer
Dishwasher
Cabinets
Mixer
Toaster
Kettle
Pans
Chairs/table
China
Cutlery
Glass
Curtains
Floor covering
Vacuum cleaner
Other
Sitting room
Carpets
Curtains
Sofa/suite
Chairs
Tables
Lamps
Cabinets
Shelves
Other
Bedrooms
Beds
Bedding
Dressing tables
Wardrobes/chest of drawers

Cosmetics
Carpets
Curtains
Other
Bathroom
Medicine and toiletries
Cabinets
Carpets
Scales
Other
Garage
Tools
Garden furniture
Workbench
Sports equipment
Bicycles
Other
Miscellaneous
Clothes
Luggage
Toys
Sports equipment
Other

High risk articles total
Other contents total
Grand total

Remember that when you use this list, you should write down the cost of buying a brand new item in the shops, not the second-hand value. Each year when you renew your insurance, you should update the values.

There are two other ways of covering your contents . Some companies simply set an upper limit for the total value of the contents, with a simplified value checklist, while others set an overall value of your contents based on the size of your home.

Rates for insurance vary tremendously – some insurers will be cheap on basic insurance but expensive if, say, you keep a valuable violin in the house, while others will give cheap 'All Risks' cover. Different companies offer different rates according to where you live – another reason to shop around.

When you buy contents insurance, you should compare cover and prices closely, and do the same every year when you renew. Premiums tend to rise with inflation, but if your renewal rate is higher than this, you may be able to find cheaper cover elsewhere.

Car insurance

You only need third party insurance to drive legally on the public roads, but for more expensive vehicles it is worth getting more comprehensive cover. The cost of insuring a car depends on:

- The make and model of car
- The size of its engine
- The car's age
- Your age and experience
- Your driving record (whether or not you have committed motoring offenses)
- The area where you live
- Your job
- Whether you use a car immobilizer and/or an alarm

Motor insurance is a price-sensitive and highly competitive business, so unless you fall into one of the high-risk categories (for instance if you buy a sports car, or if you are a young driver), you have a wide range of insurance to choose from. You can contact insurance brokers who will search on computers for quotes from different companies,, but you will still find that the 'cheapest' quotes will vary, even using the same computer system. Various societies and specialist groups offer bargain insurance to their members – if you are a policeman, for instance, you will often be able to obtain cheap insurance through your professional organisations.

Some insurers operate a 'no-claims' bonus which offers discounts of up to 35% on their published rates. Usually the discounts are on a sliding scale, increasing over five years if there are no claims. This is not the same as 'no blame', however; if your car is damaged in a car park, for instance, and you cannot find the driver, you may have to claim on your own insurance and lose your no-claims discount. You may be able to take your no-claims bonus with you if you switch insurers, and some companies simply offer you a low standard rate based on your safety record, with no discount.

Your basic insurance may not cover you if you take the car abroad; you will normally need to obtain a 'Green Card' for foreign driving, which may or may not be free from your insurer. You may need to buy special insurance for driving in certain countries. In Spain, for example, you need insurance to pay for a court 'bail bond' if you have an accident – otherwise, you could go to jail until the trial, even if the accident was not your fault.

Travel insurance

Holiday insurance is a low-cost item, so not many policies give you much choice in the cover they offer. If you are going on a package holiday to Spain, or skiing in the Alps, you will pay a set amount per week for a standard insurance package. If you want to go away for longer, or travel in less-frequented countries, you will have to contact a specialist insurance broker. The standard package will include the following.

Third party claims

The largest figure in most policies is 'personal liability cover' which may offer as much as £1 million against claims from others for injury or damage to their property.

Medical expenses

Medical expenses are usually also covered for a large figure, ranging from £250,000 to £5 million; the amount of the cover makes little difference to premiums. Medical insurance will cover you against bills incurred while you are on holiday from hospitals or doctors, but only for emergencies. It will not usually pay for 'pre-existing conditions'; if for example, you have a kidney complaint and need regular dialysis, you must pay for it yourself while abroad. If you have a chronic illness, you should disclose this when you fill in the insurance proposal. Another common exclusion is pregnancy; this can be a problem if you go on holiday unaware that you are pregnant and incur medical expenses relating to it. You should check the terms of your policy to see if you are covered in this eventuality.

Repatriation on death

Travel insurance generally covers the cost of repatriating your body if you die abroad – the cost of doing this privately can be high.

Common exclusions

Many activities are excluded under most travel policies; these include suicide, drug-related illness, AIDS-related conditions, motorbike injuries and injuries relating to a wide range of sports. You may be able to get special insurance for some sports activities, such as skiing.

Cancellation

If your holiday is delayed by more than 24 hours by adverse weather or a strike, you should be able to claim for the whole cost of the holiday. If you miss your plane for some other reason, you may be able to claim some money towards getting another plane.

Disablement

Most packages will pay out a lump sum if you suffer serious injury.

Theft

The normal limit of compensation is around £1,000, of which about £250 may be for lost cash or credit cards. If you are taking valuable items abroad, you should insure them specially. You may only be able to claim if you report the theft at a local police station and obtain a copy of the theft report.

You can take out insurance each time you go abroad, but if you travel regularly it will be cheaper to take out a policy that covers you all the year round. Travel insurance is a good example of a case where the potential loss to you is much greater than the premiums – being landed with huge medical bills in a foreign country is no fun at all.

— Claiming on an insurance policy —

Insurance companies expect claims – it is in the nature of their business. Many people are afraid of claiming but most claims are simple procedures as long as you stick to certain rules which are outlined below. Very large claims are almost never easy, and in such cases you will probably need to pay for professional help to pursue your claim.

Many of the better-known insurance companies pride themselves on running efficient and speedy claims services; often their policies are relatively expensive. Cheaper insurance deals may cause you more difficulty if you have to claim. Here are the main points to remember when you claim.

- Obtain a claim form from the company and fill it in correctly; many claims are delayed because the claimant does not complete the form properly.
- Keep copies of all your correspondence, including the claim form.
- Make sure that you claim as soon as possible after the event has occurred. If you leave it for too long to claim, the insurer could delay the claim or even disallow it.
- You need to prove the losses you are claiming for; get and keep all receipts for money that you pay out. Claims for repairs to property or vehicles should be backed up by estimates from reputable repairers. Your insurer will tell you if they need more than one estimate.
- Always report thefts to the police; if you don't the insurer has a sure get-out.
- Don't pay for repairs until your insurer has given you the go-ahead. In case of major floods and storms, many insurers will announce that all their clients should go ahead with emergency repairs.

Insurers suffer from a large number of fraudulent claims, some of which they pay out on to avoid adverse publicity. Your best protection against having a claim disallowed is:

- Making sure that you understand the exclusions of the policy before you buy it
- Making sure that you fill in the proposal form truthfully, and including all relevant facts.

Making larger claims

Substantial claims are almost always investigated by the insurer. The insurer may appoint a 'loss adjuster', who is an outside expert who will inspect the damage and collect evidence which may count against you. If, say, your house burnt down and the loss adjuster found that you had been making inflammable chemicals in your bedroom, the insurer might not pay out.

You can't employ a loss adjuster yourself, but you can use a loss assessor, who usually works on a percentage of the expected payout. The loss assessor works in the same way as a loss adjuster, but is representing your case.

Insurers don't have to take any notice of the reports of loss adjusters or loss assessors, but if both sides come up with similar estimates, the chances are that the insurer will make a settlement. If the estimates are far apart, you may be able to go to arbitration, but if the insurer is unwilling to accept this, your only option is to go to court.

Claiming on a life assurance policy (see pages 127–131) can be a problem. Deaths from AIDS and drug-related problems have made insurers stickier about claims in recent years, and you may find that the company investigates the cause of death thoroughly. There have been problems with fraudulent death certificates in certain countries, so if the insured person dies abroad, the investigation could be protracted. In such cases, you will need to employ the services of a solicitor to argue your case.

Another problem with large claims is 'under-insurance'. When you buy insurance, you should make sure that the total value of what is insured is covered. This particularly affects buildings and contents insurance, as discussed on page 119. Suppose, for example, you have insured your total house contents for £50,000 but the true replacement value is £100,000. If you then lose half of your house contents in a fire, the insurer will pay you only half (£25,000) of the replacement value, arguing that you have only bought half the insurance you needed.

Protection products

In the following sections we will survey the range of what are known in the trade as 'protection products'.

They are *not* primarily investments, although they may have some investment element. If you want to start investing, learn about bonds, unit trusts, shares and business in general. Insurance salespeople are not supposed to mislead you by over-emphasising the investment element in some insurance policies, but some have done so.

Some of these products are excellent, while others are less so – the main thing to remember about them is that they are commercial products sold by companies to make profits. Insurance companies have enormous economic power in Britain and are deeply embedded in the fabric of the economy; sometimes you may find yourself effectively being forced to buy insurance in order to obtain what you want, such as a mortgage, which may not necessarily be insurance of the best type or value.

Basic life assurance – 'term assurance'

Term assurances are the oldest and simplest form of life insurance. They are also the cheapest form of life cover. They guarantee to pay out a sum of money if the person insured dies within a given time. You choose the length of time (the 'term') when you take out the policy – it can be anything from a few days to 50 years or more.

The idea of life insurance is that it protects people who would lose out financially if you died unexpectedly. Usually this means your family, but it could be your employer, a business partner or a mortgage lender. If you are single and no-one would suffer financially if you died, you don't need life insurance.

Term assurance policies can be for one person only, or for two or more. Often a husband and wife can take out a policy which, in the event of one or the other of them dying, will provide money for the survivor to support the family, or if they both die, money for the children.

Since no benefit is paid if you outlive the expiry date of the policy, term assurance is only appropriate for temporary protection. It is not suitable as protection that will last for the whole of your life. Typical examples of how you might use term assurance include:

- Life cover for a family on holiday overseas for a few weeks.
- Life cover for a family until the children have grown up.
- Life cover to pay off a mortgage or other loan in the event that you die before paying it off.
- If you are wealthy and your estate might be liable for heavy inheritance tax (see page 77), you can get seven-year term assurance policies which are designed to give cover against possible inheritance liabilities in the event of your early death.

No-one can take out any form of life assurance policy unless they have an 'insurance interest' in the life of the person being insured. Everyone has unlimited insurable interest in their own lives and in that of their spouse, but in all other relationships insurable interest is limited to the financial loss the assurer would incur on the death of the person whose life was assured – this rule is to prevent unscrupulous business practices.

The main types of term assurance are:

- Level term assurance
- Decreasing term assurance
- Convertible term assurance
- Family income benefit
- Renewable term assurance

Level term assurance

With this type, the amount paid out if you die remains unchanged throughout the period ('term') of the policy. At the end of the term the contract expires without value because there is no investment or profit element.

The policy can be used to repay a loan on your death. It is appropriate if you have a loan which has fixed capital value which remains the same throughout its term. Provided the level term assurance is for the same period and amount as the loan, you can insure fully against your early death.

Decreasing term assurance

This is generally the cheapest form of life cover. Every year you live, the initial amount you have insured for gets less, usually on a fixed scale, until at the end of the term it is at zero.

Mortgage protection assurance is probably the most common type – it is used with repayment mortgages to make sure that the capital balance outstanding is repaid if you die before the end of the mortgage term.

It is used to pay off repayment mortgages in the event of your death. If the mortgage is in joint names, the policy should cover both your lives, paying out the full sum if one of you dies so that the other is able to pay off the mortgage on the home.

It is important to realise that these policies don't guarantee to pay off the mortgage exactly. The policy will have a schedule of decreasing benefits payable which assumes a given rate of mortgage interest. If interest rates average more than the level assumed in the schedule, there could be a shortfall in the money needed to clear the mortgage debt if you died.

Term assurance	Main feature	Common uses	Profit element?	Relative cost
Level term	The amount paid out if you die stays the same throughout the term	Repaying a loan if you die, if the amount of the loan doesn't reduce (e.g., where you only pay interest)	No	Cheap
Decreasing term	The amount paid out if you die reduces over time	Mortgage protection; protecting children you support	There could be a surplus or a shortfall depending on future interest rates	Cheapest
Convertible term	Option to convert to 'whole of life' (endowment) assurance	If you think you will need 'whole of life' insurance later (see Figure 9.3)	Depends on policy	10% more than level term assurance
Family income benefit	Income for your family if you die	If you think the people you support would not be able to handle a large capital sum if you died	No	Cheaper
Renewable term	Guaranteed option to renew at the end of the term	If you think you might need 'whole of life' insurance later	Depends on policy	About 10% more than level term assurance

Fig 9.2

Convertible term assurance

This type of policy gives you an option to convert the policy into a permanent assurance – that is, 'whole of life' assurance or 'endowment' (see page 131) – in the future. The option limits the amount insured on the new policy to the same amount as in the original term assurance policy. You must exercise the option before the policy expires, and you are usually allowed to convert some or all of the sum.

This kind of assurance costs about 10% more than a non-convertible policy. The key benefit to you is that you cannot be refused the right to take out the new policy, whatever your state of health when you are converting. You can even exercise this option if you are dying on the day before the policy expires.

If you convert to a permanent assurance, the premium will increase both for your age and for the higher cost basis of the new policy. You should take out convertible assurance where you need to keep your options open for the future. Without it, if you became ill you might find it very expensive or impossible to take out new life assurance.

Family income benefit

This sounds as if it is something to do with the state benefit system, but in fact it is a product like all the others. Under this contract, the benefit is paid from the time of your death (if you die) until the end of the term you have selected. The benefit is an income which is paid monthly, quarterly or annually. It is intended to provide an income for your family if you die unexpectedly. Spouses can take out policies jointly.

Your family can exchange the income for a lump sum if you die. You can arrange a policy with an increasing or escalating benefit to counteract the effects of inflation. The increase is a prearranged annual percentage figure which raises the income benefit payable in the event of a claim.

After a claim, the percentage increase may stop, so that the benefit is effectively frozen at the level at the time of your death, or the benefit may continue to increase during the remaining term of the policy.

The main reason why people take out family income benefit insurance is if they are supporting a spouse or children who are not use to handling money. It may be worthwhile if you have a young family with a low overall income and you decide that it would be better, if you died unexpectedly, to have the insurance company pay your family an income rather than give them a large sum of money that they might not be able to look after properly.

Renewable term assurance

This is very similar to convertible term assurance except that you have the option to exchange the original term assurance for another at the end of the term. Again, your premiums may go up, but you have the advantage that you are guaranteed that you can get life assurance whatever your state of health when you renew.

The coming of AIDS has meant that this kind of policy is now usually only available for five years or so. Generally, any option to renew is limited to policies expiring at age 60 or 65.

—— 'Whole of life' insurance ——

This kind of insurance guarantees to pay the amount assured on your death, whenever it happens. It gives you cover for the people you support whenever this becomes necessary. Since the insurance company will have to pay out on all policies, whole life assurance is more expensive than term assurance policies. In return you receive a guarantee that on some day in the future, there will be a return from the policy. There is controversy over whether whole of life insurance is useful except for inheritance tax planning.

The arguments for whole of life assurance

Some people say that whole of life assurance should be the foundation of everyone's financial planning. Since the older you get, the more likely you are to die or become ill, so, the argument goes, the sooner you can afford to take out a whole of life policy the better. It is argued that it is better to have too much cover than to risk being without full cover when you need it. Life assurance planning means protecting the people you support against events that may happen and you need a wide range of options. Many insurance providers also claim that having as many benefits as possible in one package makes administration easy and easier to understand, and that the policy will provide a reasonable return in the long term.

Whole of life Insurance	Main feature	Advantages	Disadvantages
Without profits	A guaranteed sum when you die – but this kind of policy is rarely on offer	–	The sum paid when you die is not protected against inflation
With profits	A guaranteed sum when you die, whenever that is, plus investment profits while you are still alive	A safe long-term savings plan combined with life insurance	The money you get if you surrender the policy early is greatly reduced

Fig 9.3

The arguments against whole of life assurance

The counter argument is that life assurance should be kept separate from investment. The idea is that you should take out separate insurance for each separate need. Life assurance policies do not provide such good investment returns as unit trusts and PEPs, for instance, which get more favourable tax treatment. Life assurance policies that are surrendered early will return less than the same amount invested in a unit trust. The surrender value for some years is less than the contributions that have been invested.

There is an active market in some types of second-hand policy. This is because a very high proportion of people taking out some types of policy find that they are unable to keep up the payments after a few years; when they are offered a low surrender value by the insurance company, they take it to a specialist broker who sells it to another investor who will pay a higher price to take over the payments. Thus, if you are considering saving through a life policy, you might get a better deal by buying someone else's than by taking out your own. You can find out about the details of the second-hand policy market in magazines such as *Money Management*.

In recent years, government policy and the regulatory influence have favoured the idea of keeping insurance separate from investment. All too often, whole of life policies have been wrongly sold as savings plans, when the purchaser would have been better off investing in, say, unit trusts. The high commission levels that salespeople have been paid on whole of life policies have attracted criticism.

Whole of life assurance is long term. It looks ahead to a person's needs when general economic investment conditions may be different; it is concerned with guarantees and this restricts investment growth. It is not suitable if you need to save and not insure, and it is not the best solution if you need several forms of insurance protection but are on a relatively low income.

Features

Since the insurance company must pay out whenever you die, there is an investment element built into the premium. Over the years, this should build a substantial investment reserve for the policy. You can use this to preserve benefits for some years after you stop paying the premiums (say, at retirement) or you can take it in cash. In the recent past, some salespeople have exaggerated this possibility – the investment reserve builds so slowly that for many years the cash values are low. If you want to invest through an insurance policy there are many much better forms of policy with regular premiums you pay throughout your life until a given age such as 60 or 85. Equally, policies can be paid for by a single lump sum to produce life assurance bonds, often called 'investment bonds'.

Most whole of life policies include additional options, such as guaranteed insurability, convertibility to another form of policy, critical illness cover and double accident benefit.

In practice there are few limits to the basic benefit for most people. Most companies would query a proposal for abnormally large amounts of cover, however, in case you had a hidden reason for expecting to claim. If you have bad health, a dangerous job or play a dangerous sport, you will find that different companies will offer you different deals with different restrictions.

Most policy options do have restrictions. Typically many options cannot be added to policies if you are older, or the option benefit ceases at a given age. There is always a maximum limit for cover for critical illness.

Without profits policies

These provide a guaranteed sum assured at death. The amount of cover chosen at the outset remains unchanged throughout the policy's life. These policies are rarely on offer these days because they are not protected against inflation.

With profits policies

In return for paying a higher premium, you receive:

- a guaranteed sum
- a share of the investment profits
- a share of the investment profits of the life fund.

The main purpose of a life fund is to accumulate enough money to pay all the guaranteed benefits when they fall due. Your contributions, minus the charges, are invested to achieve this and to provide a strong reserve to protect your benefits against possible future falls in the value of the fund.

With profits policies can be a good investment if you are a cautious investor who wants to take on a long-term savings plan. You should not take out such a policy, or purchase a second-hand one, unless you are very confident that you can keep up the payments for the full term.

Health insurance

In the section we will look at:

- Permanent health insurance
- Critical illness insurance
- Medical expenses insurance
- Long-term care insurance

Permanent health insurance

Income benefit is paid out if you are unable to work because of sickness or injury. The payments start at the end of an initial waiting period, which may be 4, 13, 26 or 52 weeks, and is paid until:

- you return to work, or
- the policy term expires, or
- you die.

Permanent health insurance and medical expenses insurance are often available through your employer or an association as group schemes. One of the major benefits of group schemes is 'free cover' where many people who might not otherwise be eligible for the insurance get a degree of cover. Group schemes may be associated with your company's pension scheme. If you cannot get insurance through a group scheme of some kind, you may find the premiums are expensive.

Features

Different companies have different definitions of disability. Generally you must demonstrate that you are totally unable because of sickness or accident to follow your own occupation or any other for which you are suited. The main features of these policies are:

- A regular income during long-term disability
- Permanent cover by the insurance company
- Benefits that may be level or may increase at a given rate
- Proportionate benefit if you are in part-time work and your earnings are reduced

Health insurance	Main feature	Common uses	Exclusions?	Relative cost
Permanent health insurance	Income if you become ill and are unable to work	Ideal if your employer pays for it!	Numerous	Cost greatly depends on the type of job you do
Critical illness insurance	A sum of money if you get a serious disease, such as • a heart attack • cancer • a stroke	If you are concerned that you might live for a long time after getting a serious disease	Depends on your medical history	Cheapest
Medical expenses insurance	Medical treatment outside the NHS	Ideal for anyone if their employer pays for it!	Depends on your age and medical history	High; can be cheaper in some areas of the country
Long-term care insurance	Money if you have to care for someone who cannot care for themselves	If you think you may have to care for an elderly relative	Depends on what the person can and cannot do for themselves	Medium

Fig 9.4

- Proportionate benefits if you take a lower paid job because of the disability

These policies aim to replace earnings you lose through sickness or injury without reducing your financial incentive to return to work. All policies stipulate a maximum income benefit limit, which is usually around 75% of your average monthly earnings in the year before you became sick or were injured. When calculating the 75% limit, the company will take into account any other health insurance policies you have and often state benefits such as statutory sick pay as well.

Statistics show that women are more likely on average to suffer ill health during working ages than men, so the insurance premiums are higher for a woman than a man of the same age and occupation.

Policy exclusions

These vary widely between different companies. Almost no policies will pay out if you develop AIDS. Other common exclusions are:

- Intentional self-inflicted injury
- If you become sick or are injured because of alcohol or drugs other than prescribed by a registered medical practitioner
- If you become sick or are injured because of an act of war or invasion, whether declared or not
- If you become sick or are injured when participating in a criminal act
- If you become sick or are injured during pregnancy, childbirth or because or any later complications
- If you become sick or are injured in a flying accident when you are not a fare-paying passenger

Your occupation

Your job is a key element in the pricing and underwriting of permanent health insurance. Often the company will categorise your job in a class ranging from 1 to 4, with 1 representing the lower-risk jobs (administrative and professional) and class 4 the highest. There is a big difference between the premiums charged between class 1 and class 4, and there are some jobs which are uninsurable. If you change your job, some companies will continue the cover regardless, while others reserve the right to cease cover. There are two main kinds of policy.

- Pure protection policies, which are similar to term assurance in that there is no investment element within the premium. If the policy comes to an end without your ever having made a claim, you will not receive a surrender value.

- Unit-linked policies, now increasingly common, which are unit-linked whole of life policies but with the only benefit provided being health insurance cover paid for monthly cancellation units. In the event of death or early surrender, the value of units under the policy minus any charge deducted by the company is available as a surrender value. This is not likely to be much, though, so you should not buy this type of insurance because of it.

Policies usually expire at age 60 or 65.

Critical illness insurance

This is sometimes called 'dread disease cover'. It pays out if you are diagnosed as having certain specified critical illnesses. Due to the advances in medicine, many people who suffer major life-threatening illnesses such as a heart attack or a stroke actually live on for a relatively long time, but are unable to continue working and often need expensive on-going specialist treatment.

In order to be accepted for critical illness insurance you will need to give your full medical details and family medical history. The insurers will assess the risk and accept or decline to insure you as they choose. If you are turned down for critical illness cover, you may still be accepted for life assurance; for example a proposal may be declined because you have a family history of heart disease, but if you are currently healthy you may be perfectly acceptable for life assurance. The range of diseases covered has increased and normally includes:

- heart disease
- strokes
- kidney failure
- cancer.

Critical illness insurance is available as an add-on to a unit-linked whole of life policy, and is also an option for endowment and term assurances. The capital sum is paid on death or the diagnosis of one of the specified medical conditions. The amount paid out is usually restricted to between £100,000 and £250,000 and may well be reduced by the amount of benefit you are receiving from other critical illness policies, if you have any. Often this type of policy is taken out as a protection against becoming ill while you have a mortgage – the policy would pay it off.

Medical expenses insurance

This covers you if you want private medical treatment outside the NHS system, giving you more choice over using specialists, timing treatments and which hospital to use. The cost of medical treatment varies throughout the country. For example, costs are very high in central London and in many hospitals in large cities. Thus the price of the insurance will vary depending on where you are likely to receive treatment. In-patients' cover provides:

- hospital charges
- specialist fees
- additional costs such as ambulance fees and nursing fees.

The contracts are renewable annually and premiums increase with your age. In most cases, you can get a discount on your premiums. For example, some companies give a discount to people who also take out a permanent health insurance contract. Others give discounts to members of certain professions or if you have not made any claims under your medical insurance policy.

Fears over the future of the NHS have made a number of people take out medical expenses insurance. The premiums are high and increase with age, which have deterred many others. The ideal solution is if you can get your employer to pay for it!

Long-term care insurance

The first schemes were introduced in the early 1990s; they are designed to cover the cost of caring for an elderly person.

The published population statistics show the need for this kind of insurance because:

- people are generally living longer
- over half the population aged 65 and over have a long-standing illness
- between 10% and 15% of these people will become immobile.

There are two types of long-term care insurance:

- policies where you make regular contributions
- policies paid for by a lump sum investment, possibly for the sale of a house if you move into a nursing home.

Generally a claim is paid when someone is unable to carry out a number of daily activities, often referred to as activities of daily living, which include things like:

- feeding oneself
- washing and bathing
- dressing
- using the toilet
- mobility
- continence.

Most companies will only accept a claim if a person cannot perform at least two of these activities.

—— General protection insurance ——

Redundancy insurance

This aims to replace your income if you are made redundant. In practice, it is rarely available except as a protection for your mortgage interest payments. It could be a sensible insurance if you are taking out a mortgage since it protects against repossession if you are made redundant and can't pay the repayments. Since the insurer's risks are high, most benefits will be hedged with restrictions and limitations, which you need to understand since they affect the amount you would receive if you claimed.

Redundancy insurance is too risky for most insurers; the recession and the drive for business efficiency have greatly increased the probability that people will be made redundant and have a period of unemployment before finding new work. Also people tend to get this insurance when they have reason to believe that they may be made redundant.

Personal accident and sickness insurance

This is fairly simple; the sum insured will be paid if you suffer an accident or are off work due to sickness. The contracts are usually taken out on an annual basis.

You are assessed at each renewal date by the insurance company and you will have to give them full details of any health problems that you have suffered within the last 12 months. The insurer will then decide whether to continue or decline the cover. However, you can get this insurance for short periods, for example as part of the insurance cover under a holiday insurance scheme. Generally the following are covered:

- Death
- Permanent disablement
- Loss of an eye or a limb
- Permanent total disablement

Personal accident and sickness insurance

This is available on both a group and an individual basis. A group scheme might consist of a firm's employees, the members of a social club or a sports association. Policies are renewable on an annual basis and do not provide permanent cover. The accident cover can be confined to specific activities, such as the work that you do, playing certain sports, or travelling.

These policies are relatively cheap compared with permanent health insurance but do not link benefits to your income and do not provide permanent cover. However, they are of great value if you need to cover a one-off event in an activity which is not covered by other insurances, or if you might have to take legal action in order to get redress for an injury or occupational illness.

Sickness and accident insurance is governed by precise definitions, and you should be aware of the exclusions and limits before buying. It is important to understand the conditions that would make you only eligible for partial payment, particularly if it is a small percentage of the full benefit.

Surrender values

Most kinds of protection policies don't have a surrender value. The premiums you pay are simply for the cover you receive and the expenses of the company you buy it from. Sometimes, a unit-linked protection policy will provide a small surrender value after a few years, but this rarely amounts to a significant sum compared with current investment growth rates.

By definition, term assurance never has a surrender value. If you stop paying the premiums the policy lapses. You will often have an opportunity to revive the policy within 12 months of discontinuing it if you pay the outstanding premiums and can give evidence of continued good health.

Whole of life policies acquire surrender values because of the investment element in the premium. A policy only begins to acquire a surrender value after an initial period, which may be anything up to five years after it begins. It will be a long time before any surrender value is more than the total premiums you have paid. For this reason, you should not buy whole of life policies if you are saving for the short term.

—— Choosing an insurance policy ——

Here's a checklist of points you should be sure of before buying any insurance.

- Does the product meet your main need?
- Do you really need the flexibility to change the product if your circumstances change? Flexibility usually involves extra cost.
- Check whether you can escape the contract without much loss if you find later that you don't need the insurance or can't afford it.
- Do you understand the exclusions and limitations if you had to make a claim?
- Can you really afford the insurance?
- Have you compared this type of insurance with other types which might also cover you for what you want?
- Have you checked if you can get cheaper insurance through group cover from your employer, trade association or some other society?
- Have you told the truth on your application? If you haven't, you may find that your insurance is invalid and you have wasted the money you have paid in premiums.
- Have you shopped around between companies and brokers?

EXAMPLE FOR YOUNG FAMILIES

Suppose you are a young couple in your twenties, working and with small children. You might consider:

- Level or convertible term assurance
- Family income benefit
- Universal whole of life assurance

When comparing the policies, the factors that you need to take into account include:

- the surrender values
- the cost of premiums
- the charging and commission structure (how much are the sales-people and middle man making?)
- the tax treatment of the premiums and benefits.

You may have needs that can only be met by a particular type of insurance. For instance, if you feel you need income protection against the possibility of long-term sickness or injury, only permanent health insurance can do the job, either as a stand-alone policy or as an option benefit under a universal whole of life policy.

10
AN INTRODUCTION TO PENSIONS

Pensions were invented to protect people from themselves. The underlying principle is simple enough; pensions are a way of saving money out of your income (combined with a state subsidy and, for employees, an employer's contribution), so that you will have enough money to live on when you retire. States encourage people to make pension arrangements to prevent them becoming destitute in old age through lack of foresight – at least, that's the theory. In practice, large numbers of retired people still suffer from inadequate incomes, so it is unwise to ignore the intricacies of the pensions system. The rules on pensions have become so complicated that few people really understand them – witness the current scandal over the high-pressure selling of certain pension products in the 1980s.

You will need to get professional advice about your pension, and also to read one of the many books available which deal exclusively with pensions (see Bibliography). In this chapter we will look at:

- Why bother with a pension?
- When should you start your pension?
- Aren't there other ways of saving for retirement?
- How does inflation affect pensions?
- Different kinds of pension
- What pensions am I eligible for?
- State pensions
- Occupational schemes
- Personal pensions
- Pension transfers
- Deciding on how much pension you need
- Pension mortgages

- Investment risk
- Annuity rates

—— Why bother with a pension? ——

Many people go through life without ever thinking of the future. No-one can say that this is wrong, as long as you appreciate what may happen once you have become old and unable to work. There are a great many powerful reasons why you should invest in pensions. As you can see from the table below, pensions grow much faster than a bank investment.

The cumulative value of a pension fund

This shows the cost of delaying the time you start making pension contributions, based on making a contribution of £1,000 a year at four different ages.

Age when payment started	Accumulated value of the fund at age 65
44 years 11 months	£145,607
49 years 11 months	£76,545
54 years 11 months	£32,200
59 years 11 months	£9,223

Source: *Equitable Life Assurance Society*

You might think that if you delayed the time you started a pension by five years it would simply reduce the value of the pension fund by £5,000 plus five years' loss of interest, but it has also lost the benefit of having the funds growing tax free over the whole time you are saving. Thus, if you started contributing at 45 rather than at 50, you would create an extra £70,000 (roughly) by the time you reached the male retirement age of 65.

If you are going to save money until you are older, it makes sense to do it through the tax-efficient means of a pension. All the money you put in receives full tax relief at either 25% or 40%. It then grows completely free of all tax. When you come to retire you can take a large proportion of the fund as a tax-free cash sum. The pension income itself is taxable, however.

When should you start your pension?

You can't start a pension too soon; the longer you wait before starting, the less you will get out when you retire. By the time you are 30, it is a good idea to have started. Younger people, and people with families, may need all the money that they are earning now, so if you are in this position, don't be too worried – the world isn't going to come to an end if you start your pension a little later in life.

Aren't there other ways of saving for retirement?

Although pensions are very tax efficient, they are not the only way to save for retirement. Your objective should be to accumulate the largest amount of capital by the time you retire from work, so that you can receive as much income as possible after you retire. The tax advantages of pensions over other forms of savings (see page 145) give pension contributions a head start, but pensions have some disadvantages.

- Pension contributions are effectively 'locked in'. You can't usually withdraw any money before your retirement age.
- When you retire, only a relatively small part of the pension fund can be taken out as cash. The bulk of the fund has to be taken as income.
- The pension income stops when you (or in some cases your spouse) die; this is different from a capital sum which you have saved in some other way, because in the latter case you can leave the money to your children or others when you die.
- There are limits to the amount you can contribute to a pension fund – broadly, 15% of your income if you are an employee, and 17.5%–40% if you are self-employed, subject to your age and overall 'capping'.

Applying the principle of not putting all your eggs in one basket, there is a good argument for not relying solely on your pension; saving schemes over which you have more control, such as PEPs and Qualifying Life Policies, may also be worth having.

How does inflation affect pensions?

What you really want from a pension is money that you can spend in real terms. It is no good having pension income of £1,000 per month if that is the price of a cup of tea when you retire! What you want is £1,000 per month in real terms – in other words, you need a sum of money that takes inflation into account.

Unfortunately, no-one knows exactly what future rates of inflation will be. It is all based on estimates. Life assurance companies often project forward at rates of 6% and 12% growth. This produces astronomical pension figures for young people, so it is confusing if you are told that paying in £50 a month will produce a pension of £100,000 in 30 years' time. If inflation were to average 7% per year for the next 30 years, then £100,000 would be worth only £12,277 in today's terms.

What you should do is to ask your pension provider to give you figures based on a real rate of return of, say, 3% or 4%. This means that you are assuming that your pension fund will grow at 3% or 4% more than inflation, rather than 6% or 12%. This will give you a better idea of what you should contribute to get an adequate pension.

The different kinds of pension

The main sources of pension are:

- the state scheme (the basic state pension and SERPS)
- employers' occupational pension schemes
- personal pension schemes taken out by individuals.

With one exception (see page 156) you can't, if you are a member of an occupational scheme, take out a personal pension as well, and conversely if you have a personal pension and then wish to join an employer's occupational scheme, you must stop contributing to your personal pension. In general, such changes don't mean that you actually lose what you have already paid into a scheme.

It is not unusual to change your employment status several times during your career; at one time you might be an employee in an occupational scheme, at another you might be employed by a company which has no pension provision and at other times you might be self-employed and ineligible for occupational pension schemes. This means that many people end up with a collection of small pensions, which may include the following.

- Pensions preserved in the schemes of previous employers.
- Pensions that have been transferred into pension products that are specifically designed to hold the 'transfer' (e.g. capital) value.
- Several different personal plans.
- Self-employed retirement annuities.

— What pensions am I eligible for? —

Apart from the basic state pension, which almost everyone will be eligible for, the main difference is between whether you are employed or self-employed.

If you are employed

Not all employers provide pension schemes and, among those that do, the level of pension benefits provided varies considerably. Occupational pension schemes can contract-out all their members and private individuals can contract-out through an appropriate personal pension plan. Thus most employees retiring in the UK will have two pensions, either the basic state pension and SERPS, the basic state pension and an occupational pension, or the basic state pension and a personal pension.

If you are self-employed

The self-employed are ineligible for SERPS (see page 157) and since they do not have an employer they cannot be members of occupational schemes. Thus, if you have been self-employed for all of your working life, you will only qualify for the basic state pension unless you take out a personal pension plan, which will rarely be as good as the more generous occupational schemes.

State pensions

These were discussed in some detail in Chapter 8, but to recap, they are divided into:

- the basic state pension
- SERPS.

The basic state pension

Almost everyone in the UK can claim this when they reach the age of 60 for women or 65 for men. The weekly level of pension in 1995/96 is

Pensions if you are employed	Does your employer offer a pension scheme?	Are you unlikely to be staying in your job for more than 2 or 3 years?	Are there gaps in your National Insurance record? (Check with the DSS)	If you are a man under 40 or a woman under 35	If you are a man over 40 or a woman over 35	If your employer doesn't offer a pension scheme
State pension (basic pension and SERPS)			Check if it is advantageous to pay Class 3 contributions	If you have the choice, don't contract-out of SERPS	If you have the choice, consider contracting-out of SERPS	
Your own pension	Your employer's scheme is probably better than a personal pension, but check the details carefully with an adviser	The employer's scheme may still be better, but consider a personal pension plan				Take out a personal pension

Fig 10.1

— 149 —

Pensions if you are self-employed	Your entitlement	Do you run your own company?	Are there gaps in your National Insurance record? (Check with the DSS)
State pension (basic pension and SERPS)	You should be entitled to the basic pension, but you are not entitled to SERPS	You are covered by SERPS	Check if it is advantageous to pay Class 2 or Class 3 contributions
Your own pension	Take out a personal pension	You could take out a personal pension plan, or set up your own employer pension scheme	

Fig 10.2

Pensions if you are not working	If you have worked in the past and been a member of an occupational pension	If you have not been a member of an occupational pension in the past	Will you get a basic state pension?	Will you get SERPS?	Are there gaps in your National Insurance record? (Check with the DSS)
State pension (basic pension and SERPS)			This is related to your National Insurance record See Chapter 7, and check with the DSS	Possibly, if you have worked before and will work again; check with the DSS	Check if it is advantageous to pay Class 3 contributions, and whether you qualify for National Insurance credits and Home Responsibility Protection
Your own pension	It's probably better to save in other ways – see Chapter 5	Consider taking out a personal pension plan			

Fig 10.3

£59.15, with an additional £35.30 for a wife claiming the pension on the basis of the husband's National Insurance contribution record. Whether or not you will receive the full amount of the basic state pension depends on your National Insurance contribution record. See page 90 for more details on this pension. You can contact the DSS who should provide you with information on how you stand for the old age pension. As you approach your retirement age, the DSS will send you a statement telling you what proportion of the old age pension you have earned. If you feel that you may have earned insufficient entitlement to the state pension, it may be possible for you to catch up on missed contributions. The letter you get from the DSS should explain this.

State Earnings-Related Pension Scheme (SERPS)

If you have been an employee (but not if you have been self-employed), you may be entitled to benefits from SERPS. SERPS is a 'top up' state pension scheme into which employees who are liable to Class 1 National Insurance make contributions and receive taxable benefits from the state pension age. In total the benefits from SERPS cannot exceed 25% of your 'middle band' earnings (see page 85). This limit reduces to 20% for employees retiring after the year 2000. If you are retiring before the year 2000, the SERPS pension will be 1.25% of the middle band earnings for each 20 years after 1978. Because you have made contributions based on these earnings for many years, the state gives you, through SERPS, an additional pension based on these earnings. This can be quite a significant addition to your pension if you have been a high earner.

In calculating individual pensions, the member's best 20 years of earnings will be used after each year's earnings have been revalued upwards in line with the increase in average UK earnings up to retirement date. People retiring before 1998 will not be able to earn a full SERPS pension.

If you have been a member of a pension scheme that was 'contracted-out', then this pension scheme will have taken over responsibility for your SERPS entitlement and the Government may not provide any additional pension at all. Alternatively you may have 'contracted-out' of SERPS into your own personal pension. This means that you are now paying lower rates of National Insurance, and all the savings are being directed to your pension provider, who will have to provide all of your pension over and above the basic state old age pension.

SERPS is a very complex issue, not just on a national level but also for each individual. Don't make any moves concerning your pension without considering this issue in depth. It is a good test of how good your pension advisers are to see whether or not they understand SERPS fully. To find out how much you are entitled to under SERPS, complete a form from your local DSS office and send it to their Retirement Pension Forecast and Advice service. They will give you details of the state pension and SERPS you have built up so far, an estimate of your pension when you retire and details of how you can improve your entitlement.

Occupational schemes

Occupational schemes can only be set up by employers for the benefit of their own employees. The scheme can be very small and only include a handful of senior employees or it can include all the employees of a large group of companies. There are also federated schemes available to employees of different firms in the same industry.

Your employer decides on the eligibility for membership of the scheme, chooses its benefits and defines its rules. Your employer may pay all costs, in which case this scheme is called a 'non-contributory scheme'. Employees may be required to contribute, in which case it is called a 'contributory scheme" – normally you contribute a fixed percentage of salary deducted from your pay through your employer's payroll process; a typical contribution is 5% or 6% of salary.

Occupational pension schemes provide you with considerable tax benefits. In order to qualify for these, the scheme must conform to the rules of the Pension Scheme Office (PSO) and receive its formal approval. The PSO is the department of the Inland Revenue responsible for supervising and overseeing private pension schemes.

Public sector schemes

These include the pension schemes of nationalised industries and the statutory superannuation schemes for civil servants and other public servants such as National Health Service employees, lecturers and teachers, police officers and fire officers. Statutory superannuation schemes are unfunded and provide benefits on a pay-as-you-go basis; the pension funds of the nationalised industries hold enormous assets and are financially very powerful.

Private sector schemes

These are provided by private sector employers ranging from large public companies such as Shell or ICI to small firms, sole proprietors and partnerships (although, in all cases, only the employees can be members of a scheme). The Pension Schemes Office approval requires that private schemes not only fund their benefits but also that they can demonstrate that the fund's assets are sufficient to pay the benefits due to members both now and in the future. Funded schemes may be self-administered or insured schemes. Self-administered schemes manage their own investment of contributions to provide future benefits. They either employ their own investment specialists or they use professionals such as stockbrokers.

Insured schemes

Insured schemes are provided by life assurance and pension companies. They provide the pensions and life policies used for insured occupational schemes. Unit trust companies also run funds for sale to trustees of charities and pension funds, and offer additional voluntary contribution (AVC) policies, free-standing additional voluntary contribution (FSAVC) policies and transfer bonds.

Unapproved schemes

Since 1989 employers have been allowed to start up 'unapproved pension schemes'; these have few of the tax benefits, and the employer's contribution is taxed as if it were part of your salary.

How safe are private sector occupational schemes?

Most occupational schemes are probably perfectly safe. However, the scandal of Robert Maxwell's misuse of his employee's pension funds shows that they are not always safe. Broadly speaking, there are many good safeguards against the misappropriation of funds, but a really determined crook who controls a company may be able to find ways around them. An insured pension fund will be safer than many company-run arrangements. For example, the Policyholders Protection Act means that members of an insured scheme would be far more likely to get their pension benefits paid by seeking them from the insurer than they would if the company went into liquidation. If the employer never paid the insurance company, then he could still run off with your money, so always get regular statements of your policy values.

It is a frightening thought that your occupational pension may not be safe from the executive thieves. Remember that your pension is your money, so look after it! Make sure that you monitor all the arrangements on an on-going basis, and use an independent professional to back you up. If you think something is wrong, don't just hope that it will work out by itself – take action, both by writing to the regulatory authorities and by looking at the possibility of leaving the scheme.

Leaving your company scheme

Company schemes are not compulsory. This means that you can opt out and go for a personal pension. There are some instances when you should do this. For example, if you think you will have a very short time with the employer, say two or three years, then you may be better off in a personal pension scheme that you intend to continue funding for a long time. Generally, though, company schemes are a better deal. The employer's contribution is valuable to you, especially if you are to stay in the scheme in the medium or long term.

Additionally, some schemes have guarantees. They say that when you retire you will get 1/60th of your salary on retirement for every year that you worked. So if you worked for 30 years you will get 30/60th of your final salary, or 1/2. If you go out to a personal pension provider and try to copy those benefits you will find it very expensive indeed.

Your employer's scheme may also be index linked or have increases during the payment of the pension. This again is extremely expensive to buy in your own right. You should obtain a booklet detailing your employer's scheme rules and give it to your pension adviser. Ask him or her to put in writing a package of pension benefits which is as good as your employer's and work out the costs. You will then be comparing like with like and be able to make a sensible decision.

Death in service benefit

Most company schemes provide you with a death benefit. Ask for a 'form of nomination' so that you can put on that form the people who you would like to benefit if you die. This gives the trustees of the scheme an idea of where you would like the money to go. If you die before your spouse then you may wish to leave everything to him or her, but consider what might happen if all your family were killed in a freak accident – who would you like to have the money then?

Additional voluntary contributions (AVCs)

These are for employees whose occupational pensions are not enough. You can make extra contributions to your pension up to the tax limits through an AVC scheme, which all employer's schemes must offer. AVCs either work as a 'money purchase' scheme, which means that your contributions are invested to build up a fund of cash, or to 'buy' extra years in schemes which are based on your years of membership. Instead of using an AVC you can contribute to a 'Free Standing Additional Voluntary Contributions' scheme (FSAVC), which is separate from your employer's scheme.

Personal pensions

Many people are not able to subscribe to employers' schemes, and should take out a personal pension. In addition, it is possible to opt out of SERPS and into a personal scheme. Personal pensions came in in 1988; it was thought that a pension that you could carry with you when moving in and out of different employment situations was an important alternative to occupational pensions.

Who provides personal pensions?

These are provided by financial institutions, such as:

- banks
- building societies
- unit trust groups
- insurance companies
- friendly societies

These organisations are well regulated, and invest the vast pension funds they control very diversely in order to make them grow. Much of the money is invested in industry by means of the stock market.

The main types of personal pension

Personal pensions are governed by many complicated laws and rules. The main types of personal pension are:

- personal pension schemes
- group personal pension schemes
- FSAVCs.

Personal pension schemes

There is no limit to the amount of pension you can receive after you retire in these schemes, but there are limits to the amount of money you can contribute in any one year (see below). This limit changes according to your age, and differs according to whether you are an employee or self-employed. Normally, you can start a personal pension at any age from 18 to 75 years.

Contribution limits

The legal limit on how much you can contribute to a personal pension in any one year is calculated as a percentage of 'Net Relevant Earnings' (NRS). If you miss contributing in a year, it is possible to 'carry back' a contribution a little later – ask your adviser about this. It is also possible to 'carry forward' unused tax relief from the last six years.

If you are an employee, your NRE is your gross earnings less 'allowable business expenses', which, in practice, few people have, so your NRE will probably be your gross remuneration. If you are self-employed, your NRE is much more complicated to work out. Get your accountant to do it for you. The following table shows how much of your NRE you can contribute to your pension in any one year, according to your age.

Age at 6 April	% of NRE
35 or under	17.5
36 – 45	20
46 – 50	25
51 – 55	30
56 – 60	35
61 – 74	40

EXAMPLE FOR PEOPLE UNDER 36

Suppose you are 27 and are getting established in a career, and that your NRE is £25,000. The most you can contribute in a year to your personal pension is

17.5% of £25,000 = £4,375.

Group personal pension schemes

These are sometimes used by small firms instead of setting up an occupational pension scheme. As as employee, you have your own personal pension policy, which is portable and transferable if you move jobs, and you can use it to decide whether or not to contract-out of SERPS. You decide how much to contribute to the scheme (within the legal limits). The employer is free to contribute to your pension or not, and can contribute different amounts to different employees' schemes.

Free-standing additional voluntary contributions (FSAVCs)

These are for members of the occupational schemes who want to top up their pension. They are an addition or an alternative to using AVCs (see page 156) and give you some privacy from your employer. Most of them are linked to unit trusts, and so they have an element of risk. Whether or not they are worthwhile depends entirely on your personal circumstances, so get professional advice.

Pension transfers

People are changing their jobs more and more often, and you may find that you are leaving pension rights behind you with an employer. To help with this, all schemes must offer a transfer value where you can take a sum from your former employer's scheme and put it into your new employer's scheme or your own personal scheme. This is an area full of pitfalls and you must get quality independent advice about it.

Deciding on how much pension you need

This depends on a number of factors, including:

- your age
- your income.

Your age

Your age is an important factor in pension planning because it affects the question of how urgent it is for you to take out a pension.

- If you are, say, aged 55 and have little or no pension provision, you don't have many years in which to accumulate the necessary pension benefits, so planning a pension should be a top priority for you.

- If you are, say, 22, you may not have begun work yet, and pensions will be less of a priority than getting established in a career and finding somewhere to live.
- If you are a young person with a family and not much spare income, providing for your family may be a much higher priority than starting a pension.
- If you are a couple in your 40s or early 50s, on good incomes but still struggling with school fees and the cost of university education, you may find that it is difficult to make additional pension contributions. However, by the time you are in your 40s, there is no time to waste before taking steps to improve your pension as much as possible.

The difference between the age you are now and the age at which you want to retire gives you the length of time available in which you can contribute to a pension.

EXAMPLE

If you are 30 years old and intend to retire at 65, you have 35 years in which to build a pension fund. The contribution you should make is much lower than for someone planning the same pension but who, being aged 45, has only 20 years in which to accumulate the necessary contributions.

Pension laws take all this into account; the basis of occupational pension schemes means that joint employer and employee contributions for older employees can exceed 100% of your gross salary. Both personal pension schemes and earlier schemes allow older people to contribute higher percentages of their pensionable earnings. As we saw earlier, the maximum contribution for personal pension plans rises from 17.5% for people under 35 to up to 40% for people within the age range 61 to 74.

Your income

Your income influences your pension in two ways.

- It determines the maximum pension you can create by law.
- It affects the amount of pension contributions which you can afford to make after paying for more pressing needs.

Since most people earn more in their 30s than in their 20s, and even more as they get closer to retirement, the limit on how much you can contribute to your pension each year increases.

Limits on tax relief for pensions

As we have seen, there are limits which restrict the amount you can invest in a pension scheme. If you are in a company pension scheme, your own contribution to that scheme is limited to 15% of your earnings from that employment, including taxable benefits. The company can contribute a much greater amount but must have an eye to the final benefits payable, which must not exceed two-thirds of your final salary. (There are further restrictions for company directors.) Personal pensions have no real limits on final benefits except that the tax-free cash element cannot be more than a quarter of the total fund.

How to build up your pension

You should try to build yourself a 'pension pyramid'. At the bottom is your basic state pension, which may not be very much. Added to this is SERPS or an equivalent from a different pension scheme. Finally on top of these two should be your main pension from either your employer or from a personal scheme or from a combination of both, depending on your employment history. You don't have much control over the old age pension or SERPS, but the major part of your pyramid is down to your own funding or that of your employer.

Working out the figures

Sit down with your monthly expenditure budget and subtract all the items that you will no longer be spending money on once you have retired. For example, your mortgage should have been paid off, you will no longer be paying National Insurance, nor any pension contributions. You will not be travelling to work or be paying union dues. Your monthly expenditure budget in retirement should be smaller.

Add to your budget any increase in expenditure you can expect. For example, you may have higher heating bills if you are going to be spending more time at home, and you may use your private telephone more because you are not using the one at work. You will have more free time and may find yourself planning more holidays.

As you get older, it may become necessary to have DIY jobs done by professionals.

Once you have estimated the amount you would need if you were to retire tomorrow, then the rest is simple maths.

EXAMPLE

Imagine you currently earn £20,000 a year. You might have a take-home pay of £1,200 per month. You may decide that you'll be able to live on a monthly income of £700 in today's money after tax when you have retired. You may need a gross income of around £10,000 a year to achieve this, depending on your tax allowance. Your pension adviser should be able to calculate this figure for you; if your adviser can't do this, get another adviser.

Remember, it is no good at all planning for your pension unless you have a target. Make your pension adviser work out a target with you and make sure you understand it. If the adviser is not willing to explain and help you understand this, then you have the wrong adviser.

How much should I put into a pension plan?

Having first decided how important pension income is in your total plan, you need to decide on the actual cash amount you will contribute, based on your target income. If you are in a final salary scheme it will guarantee you a certain fraction of your salary when you retire. For this you will probably have to make a contribution but it will be much less than the actual contribution required to secure the guarantee. The bulk of the cost should be borne by your employer. In this case you need to decide how much retirement income you will need, and ask your employer for a quotation of your likely benefits. If there is a gap between what you would actually need and what you are likely to get, then you will need funds for the difference and you should ask your employer what schemes are available. Large group schemes often have very low charges that make them efficient, and special arrangements for making up for any shortfall in your requirement.

You will need to decide whether you simply make AVCs into a cash fund which will be converted into a pension when you retire, or whether you actually buy extra years in the scheme. You will undoubtedly need advice to make an important decision like this, and your Personnel Manager or the trustees of the scheme should be able to point you in the right direction. If you are seriously considering committing a reasonable proportion of your income to pension funding on this basis, it will be well worth paying £300 or so to a firm of consulting actuaries or to one of the top independent financial advisers to get to the truth.

A great many people are either in company pension schemes or have their own personal pension schemes which do not offer guarantees. In this case it should be a fairly simple matter of what you get out being based on what you put in. But pensions are surprisingly expensive.

So follow the simple steps below and you should reach a reasonable funding figure for your pension.

EXAMPLE

If you are a man wishing to retire at 60 and draw a pension of £10,000 after tax, with that pension continuing to be paid to your wife if you die first and annual increases of 5% to help counteract inflation, you will actually need a fund of £155,000. So if you are 40, you only have 20 years in which to build up those funds.

- Decide what your target pension is in today's money – for example £10,000.
- Have your adviser work out what this figure will be when you retire based on your view of inflation.
- Ask the adviser for a quotation that will produce a pension of the inflated size, assuming that the pension fund increases in value, through sound investment, at a rate of 3% or 4% above your chosen inflation figures.

This is nowhere near as complex as it sounds once you understand the principle, and if your pension adviser doesn't then change him or her. In any event, the table on page 163 gives examples of the amount you need to put into a personal pension fund in order to get any worthwhile result.

Assuming that everyone wants half-salary on retirement with 50% to their spouse on death, and also assuming that pension funds will grow at 8.5% with inflation at 5.5%, the following contributions are needed, expressed as a percentage of gross salary.

	Proposed retirement age		
Age now	**55**	**60**	**65**
30	18.55%	13.58%	9.1%
35	25%	17.7%	12.69%
40	35.71%	23.58%	16.45%
45	58.13%	33.78%	22.02%

Pension mortgages

This is simply a mortgage for which you pay only interest to the lender for the term of the loan. At the end of the term you repay the loan out of the tax-free cash you receive from your pension scheme, leaving the rest of the pension fund to provide your retirement income. This can be a very efficient way of repaying a mortgage because of the tax benefit of pensions (see page 177).

Investment risk

When you take out a pension you may link it to a wide variety of funds, from cash to the Japanese stock market. You must ask yourself what risk you want to take with your pension benefits. It will be a very serious matter if just prior to your retirement you have an October '87 type of stock market crash and find your pension is halved. This happened to many people. You should therefore make your pension a relatively medium-risk affair in the early years, perhaps in a managed fund or with a profit fund. You should then get off to a good start. As you get nearer to retirement you may like to reduce the amount of risk by gradually transferring your money into less risky funds. Once you are within five years of retirement you really should be in cash, fixed interest or with profit funds.

Quality publications such as *Money Management*, *Pensions Management* and *Planned Savings* provide a wealth of information, and will help you choose which life offices are the best on pensions.

Annuity rates

All your years of sound pension planning can be wasted if you don't understand annuity rates. These are simply the rates at which your fund is converted into a pension. If you have a fund of £100,000 and a 10% annuity rate, your pension should be £10,000 a year. With an 8% annuity rate, your pension should be £8,000, and so on. You do have a measure of control over the annuity rate. Go to an independent adviser to get the best annuity rate; the difference between the best and the worst on offer can be as much as 30%. Thus if you bought badly, you could end up with £7,000 a year instead of £10,000. Most pensions have an open market option written into the contract so that you can shop around like this and you really must do it.

Another way you can get a better rate is by delaying or hastening your retirement. Suppose that interest rates are currently 7% but the economy is going mad and everyone expects interest rates to go up – to as much as 12%. In such circumstances, it would be a good idea to wait until they have gone up so you can get a better annuity rate. Suppose interest rates are 12% but there is an election coming up and experts are predicting that rates will go down. You should convert your pension quickly before they do.

Of course, annuity rates are also based on age; this is because when you convert your pension you have a certain life expectancy. Someone retiring at 55 will have a greater life expectancy, normally, than some-one retiring at 70. So at any given time the older person will be offered the better rate. Talk to the adviser who sold you the pension in the first place and get him or her to produce a graph based on annuity rate expectations and your current age and predict the point at which you will be best off taking your pension. However, some people in company pension schemes may not have the opportunity to defer taking their pension, and must buy a 'compulsory purchase annuity'.

Summary

Here is a list of the basic points to remember about pensions.

- If possible, start your pension by the age of 30 to give your fund as much time as possible in which to grow.

- Pensions grow tax free, but your pension income is taxed after retirement.
- Normally, you can't take any money out of your pension fund before you retire. When you retire, you can only take out a fairly small amount as a lump sum – the rest has to be used to buy an annuity which will give you an income.
- Your pension stops when you (or sometimes your spouse) die, but you can bequeath your assets to whomever you want. For this reason, it makes sense to save in other ways as well as by contributing to your pension.

The main types of pension are:

- the basic state pension
- SERPS
- employers' occupational pension schemes
- personal pension schemes.

Most people will get the basic state pension; your eligibility to join the other schemes depends upon your employment status and what scheme your employer offers.

- Always get professional advice before committing yourself to a pension scheme.
- Always monitor your pension fund regularly, and satisfy yourself that it is being properly administered.
- With some pensions you can choose how they are linked to underlying investments. Make your pension a low-risk or medium-risk affair, especially in the early years.
- When you approach retirement, shop around for the best annuity rates; it may be worth hastening or delaying retirement to get a better rate.

Despite their complexity, pensions do offer an extremely sound way of providing for your old age, so take the trouble to plan carefully so that you can enjoy a worry-free retirement.

11

———— MORTGAGES ————

As the finance industry never tires of telling us, a mortgage is probably the biggest kind of loan we will ever take out. If you do it wisely, it should also be the safest and most financially rewarding money you ever borrow. Technically, the word 'mortgage' doesn't refer to the loan, but to the fact that you are offering your home as security of the loan ('mortgaging' it). To keep life simple, we will stick to the habit of calling the loan on your home a mortgage.

In this chapter we will look at:

- What is a mortgage?
- Why have a mortgage?
- The process of raising a mortgage
- How much can you borrow?
- How much do mortgages cost?
- Mortgage Interest Relief at Source (MIRAS)
- Capital and interest (repayment) mortgages
- Endowment mortgages
- Pension mortgages
- PEP mortgages
- Interest options
- Which type of mortgage should you have?
- Cost of mortgages
- Flexibility of the term
- Partial repayment
- What if you are made redundant?
- Protecting your mortgage repayments
- Using your equity
- Remortgages

What is a mortgage?

A mortgage is a contract between you and a lender where your promise to repay the debt is backed up by your agreement to provide your home as security. Mortgages have been available in one form or another for hundreds of years and will always be needed as long as people are unable to save enough money to buy a home outright when they want to. Rather than waiting for 30 years or so to save the money, it makes sense to borrow it in this way so you can buy your home now.

With the wide choice of lenders that is available today, the difficult parts of purchasing a house are deciding:

- when is the right time to buy
- how much you can borrow
- how much the loan will cost.

Only you can decide the right time to buy. Will property prices drop further? Have you got enough for a deposit? Is your job safe enough to make such a big commitment? To make this decision wisely, you will need to learn quite a lot about property, the property market and the mortgage market first. In this chapter you will be introduced to the intricacies of the mortgage market.

Why have a mortgage?

The vast majority of people who borrow money to help them pay for the purchase of a house or a flat do so because they do not have enough capital to purchase the home outright. Historically, in the UK it has been difficult to save up all the money by yourself to do this for two main reasons.

- Since the Second World War, house prices have tended to rise faster than a person has been able to save money, so people have felt that they would never be able to save enough to get onto the housing ladder.
- The cost of renting a place to live while you are saving to buy reduces your ability to save.

These pressures have, for the last 50 years or so, encouraged people to borrow all or part of the price of a house. In general, this has been a successful strategy, since house prices have outpaced inflation and most people have profited quite nicely by purchasing. Whether or not housing will produce this kind of investment return in the future is a matter for speculation; since the late 1980s house prices have fallen. There is no room here to discuss the future prospects of UK property as an investment in detail; if you want to learn about it properly, try reading *Principles of Property Investment and Pricing* by W. D. Fraser, Macmillan 1993, which is a standard textbook.

As we will see later, the Government encourages us to take out mortgages by giving us tax relief on the interest cost through MIRAS (see page 176). The amount of the relief has been reduced in recent years, however.

The process of raising a mortgage

It is generally a good idea to have saved money for a deposit before looking to buy a property. This is discussed in detail on page 174, but as a rule of thumb, try to save at least 10% of the price of the property you hope to buy. If you have only recently started earning, this may take two or three years, unless you can borrow the money from friends or relatives. Once you have the deposit, you can start looking for a home. After you have visited a large number of properties (the more the better), you will begin to get an idea of what you want. At the same time as you are doing this, you should also approach lenders, such as banks, building societies, and other financial institutions. You could also talk to a mortgage broker, but be careful in the early stages about parting with any money as a fee.

Skipping the process of negotiating the loan for the moment, we should look at what happens if your application for a loan is successful. If it is, the lender will make you an offer to lend up to a certain amount when you complete the house purchase. Almost always, this money will not be handed over to you personally. It will be sent to the solicitor acting on your behalf who will in turn pass on the full purchase price to the person who is selling the house or, more usually, to his or her solicitor. The lenders like to do it this way because they trust solicitors not to run off with the money – if they gave it straight to you, you might be tempted to do something silly!

The money you need to complete the purchase of the house must be available before the final completion date; on the final completion date, the solicitor promises to the lender to:

- complete the legal formalities to transfer the ownership of the property into your names
- 'charge' the property immediately afterwards to the lender by way of mortgage.

This means that you are not free to deal with the 'title' (ownership) to the property entirely as if it were your own. The title deeds to the property will be held safely by the lender. Your property is not charged to the lender permanently, but on a temporary basis until you have repaid the mortgage. When you have paid all the money back, the title deeds will be returned to you, and the lender will no longer have any rights over your home. In practice, of course, most people move home before they finish paying off their mortgage, so there are special arrangements to cope with this. One thing to remember is that it is expensive to buy or sell a house. As well as the interest charges, there is also a variety of fees to pay (see page 175).

How much can you borrow?

There are various types of mortgage available, but before examining these, you should try to get a grasp of why there is a limit, peculiar to you, on how much you can borrow. Unless you are rich, you can't just go and borrow £5 million to buy a luxury mansion, because the lender wants to be sure that you can pay the money back over the period you have borrowed it for. It is important to get this limit right because, among other things, it dictates the price you are able to pay for the property. If you are a first-time buyer, you will probably buy somewhere fairly cheap to begin with, with the intention of buying a bigger place later when you are earning more money. The process of progressively selling one home to buy a more expensive one is called the 'property ladder'. The amount you can borrow depends on five main factors.

- Your income
- Your liabilities
- The amount of deposit you have
- Your credit history
- Your employment status

How much can you borrow?	Varies with lender?	What points might make it difficult for me to borrow?	What points will make it easy for me to borrow?
Your income	Yes, but typically 2.5 times a couple's joint income, or 3 times the higher income plus 1 times the lower income	A low-income; self-employment with erratic income	High income in a secure job
Your liabilities	Yes – often reduces the amount you can borrow	If you have lots of unsecured debts	Debts within your means that you clear off regularly
Your deposit	Yes – but currently it should be at least 5–10% of the price of the property	If you have no deposit	The higher the deposit, the better
Your credit history	Yes	If you have been: • bankrupt, ever defaulted on a mortgage • have County Court Judgements against you	A clean credit record
Your employment status	Yes	If your work is seen as likely to make your income erratic (e.g. acting)	If you are seen to be in a line of work that is likely always to be in demand

Fig 11.1

Your income

Most lenders are happy to talk about the amount they are willing to lend you (which can vary a lot between different lenders) well in advance. The amount they will lend is usually calculated by using 'income multipliers'. You may hear phrases like 'three plus one' and 'two and a half times joint'. 'Three plus one' simply means that a lender will lend a couple three times the higher income plus one times the lower income where a couple is buying a house jointly. 'Two and a half times joint' means two and a half times the total income of a couple. A single person can borrow less than a couple because there is only one income to use for the repayments.

EXAMPLE

Suppose Carol and Rob are buying a house together. Carol earns £20,000 and Rob earns £9,000. How much can they borrow?

Using a three plus one multiplier, the maximum loan available will be:

	3 × £20,000	=	£60,000
plus	1 × £9,000	=	£9,000
	Total maximum loan	=	£69,000

Using a two and a half times joint multiplier, the maximum would be:

2.5 × (£20,000 + £9,000) = £72,500

Total maximum loan = £72,500

Suppose, however, that Carol earns £15,000 and Rob earns £14,000. Their total joint income is the same as before (£29,000), so on the two and a half times joint multiplier, their maximum loan would be the same as before, but using the three plus one multiplier:

	3 × £15,000	=	£45,000
plus	1 × £14,000	=	£14,000
	Total maximum loan	=	£59,000

The maximum loan available will be £59,000 – £10,000 less than before.

This is one reason why it pays to shop around different lenders to find who will lend you the most.

How much of your income will the lender allow you in the calculation?

Your income may come in many ways, including:

- Your salary
- Your guaranteed overtime
- Your overtime which is not guaranteed
- Commissions
- Unearned income (e.g. investments)
- Guaranteed bonuses
- Unguaranteed bonuses
- Part-time income

Each lender decides which of these parts of your total income can be taken into account when deciding how much to lend you. In general, if your income is guaranteed or you can prove that you have received it regularly, say over the last three years, the lender allows the full amount of your income to be included in the multiplier. If some part of your income is not guaranteed, the lender will either not allow it at all, or only allow a proportion of it to be taken into account.

Proof of your income

Most lenders want proof that you earn what you say do. This can take the form of the last six months' salary slips, P60s for the last two years, or an income reference, which is a questionnaire sent to your employer which asks for the details of your income and confirmation that your job is permanent. The form requires a company stamp and a signature of someone in authority in the company. If you are self-employed, you are usually asked to produce three years of audited accounts to prove your income. This is used for the income multiplier. If you do not have three years of audited accounts, sometimes a letter from your accountant will do – this varies between lenders. In both cases the lender is looking for as much security as possible in order to stop you from over-stating your income and borrowing more than you can repay.

Why do people try to borrow too much money?

It was not only in the housing boom that people tried to borrow too much – it happens all the time. One of the main reasons why people do it is that they are in a rush to buy their dream house, which always seems to be a little more than they can really afford. It is in your best interests, as well as the lender's, not to borrow more than you can afford. It is not impossible to fiddle your income statements in various ways to make it look as if you earn more than you do. My advice is – *don't*! Not only is this fraud, and you could be taken to court for doing it at a later date, but also it is foolish because you will have terrible trouble making the repayments if you have borrowed too much. Lenders hate repossessing houses almost as much as you would hate to have your house repossessed, so respect their experience in this matter.

Your liabilities

All lenders have to make sure that you can afford to repay the monthly installments without being financially overstretched. As mentioned above, if you take on too high a commitment you are in danger of not having enough money to make the repayments, especially if interest rates increase, which will push up the monthly repayments. To avoid this, the lender looks at what else you have already borrowed, including:

- amounts on credit cards
- HP agreements
- bank overdrafts
- mortgages on other properties
- tax bills owed by self-employed people.

EXAMPLE

Suppose that Jane and Jim are a couple wanting to buy a house. Jane's salary is £14,000 and Jim's is £10,000. They have an HP loan for £2,900 which will cost £69 a month for the next four years and owe £500 to a credit card company. They say that they pay off the credit card balance every month. Supposing the lender uses the 'three plus one multiplier to do the following:

- Calculate the maximum loan in the normal way
  3 × £14,000 = £42,000
  1 × £10,000 = £10,000
  Total = £52,000
- Subtract the HP loan from the total
  £52,000–£2,900 = £49,100

The lender will probably ignore the credit card loan, and offer Jane and Jim £49,100.

There are other ways of accounting for your liabilities, so this is yet another reason to shop around.

The amount of your deposit

When house prices were rising in the 1980s, many lenders were happy to lend 100% of the value of the property because they thought that the value of the property would increase, covering the debt and giving the borrower a profit. Since then, property prices have been falling, which has made lenders stop lending 100% mortgages. At present you will be unlikely to be able to borrow more than 90% or 95% of the value of the property.

The difference between the amount you owe on your mortgage and the price you would get if you sold your house is called the 'equity'. If you are, say, a second-time buyer with some equity, you will be able to borrow, but it has caused trouble for many first-time buyers who do not have a deposit. The main benefits of having a deposit are:

- Your monthly payments will be less.
- The cost of insuring against not being able to repay the loan (see page 176) will be less.
- You will have a wider choice of lenders and may be able to get better terms.

Your credit history

Lenders also check your creditworthiness. Creditworthiness used to have a sort of pseudo-moral aura around it – if you have never been badly in debt, you were somehow a better person than if you had been. This ethos still survives, but these days people are more realistic, and know that anyone can make a mistake. What lenders want to make sure of, though, is that you are not the kind of person who never stops making mistakes with their money. They may do this in several ways.

- They may interview you, to probe into whether you are trying to borrow too much. People who work in the lending industry are not known for having rich imaginations, so try not to worry them by saying or doing anything that they might think is odd.
- They may ask for a reference from your existing mortgage lender, if you have one, to see that you were good at making the repayments.
- They may ask for a reference from your landlord to see that you pay the rent on time.

- They will check to see if you are bankrupt, or have been, and whether you have any County Court Judgements (CCJs) against you for debts.

If these checks throw up something the lender doesn't like, you may be refused a loan, or only get it after a lot of explaining.

Your employment status

Lenders don't like lending to people who have job-hopped over the years and have no real track record – they prefer people who can show a steady career development with one or two employers over a number of years. This is a bit old fashioned, considering that many of us change jobs these days through no fault of own, so if you can present a good case you should be all right.

Lenders prefer to lend to people whose skills are always likely to be in demand in the labour market, for example skilled carpenters, doctors, and graphic artists. If you are, say, an actor or a rock singer, the lender may be doubtful about your ability to remain in work. The lender wants you to have a steady employment record and to seem 'stable'.

How much do mortgages cost?

As was mentioned earlier, buying and selling a house are expensive because there are a number of extra costs. These include:

- arrangement fees
- legal fees
- stamp duty
- indemnity guarantee premium
- survey fee.

Arrangement fees

If you are getting a fixed-rate loan (see page 181) in particular, you may be asked to pay the lender between £50 and £250 with the mortgage application – the fee is normally non-refundable which means that you won't get it back, which encourages you to stick with that lender so you haven't wasted the money. You shouldn't pay this fee unless you are fairly sure that you want to use the lender.

Legal fees

It is legal for you to do your own 'conveyancing', as the legal work of property transactions is called, but there can be pitfalls, so if you are a first-time buyer this is probably not a good idea. Most people use a solicitor or a licensed conveyancer to do their conveyancing, and must pay a fee. Solicitors are generally more expensive than licensed conveyancers, and their fees vary enormously – 1% of the purchase price is not uncommon. Try to use a solicitor or licensed conveyancer who has been recommended to you, and pin them down on how much their fee will be before starting the work. Part of the fee will be for formalities such as the 'local searches', which check with local authorities for matters that may affect your property, such as planned public works, and to register you as the new owner with the Land Registry.

Stamp duty

This is a tax. It is charged at 1% for properties costing more than £60,000. If you are buying a property which is a little over this figure, you may be able to avoid the stamp duty by allocating the amount over £60,00 to fixtures and fittings which come with the house, but this must be recorded in the particulars of the sale and you must prove that this is a fair value to the Inland Revenue.

Indemnity guarantee premium

Once a lender has agreed to lend you the money, they will often take out insurance against the possibility that you cannot repay the mortgage for some reason. The cost of the premium will be passed on to you. Normally this is not very much, but make sure you know how much it is before you borrow.

Survey fee

By law, building societies have to obtain a professional survey and valuation on a property which they lend money on, and you will be charged for it. Other lenders tend to do the same, although they are not required to by law. This has become a rather cosy arrangement, and some people say that lenders overcharge for this, since the basic survey is not detailed. Although you may be offered a more detailed survey under this scheme, you may well be better off commissioning your own survey from a professional surveyor of your choice. To be fair to lenders, it is important for them to check that the property is as you say it is and that there are no suspicious connections between you and the seller which the survey might pick up.

Mortgage Interest Relief at Source (MIRAS)

If you are raising a mortgage on your main residence, the Inland Revenue allows you to claim tax relief on the interest payments on the first £30,000 of the loan. The relief has been reduced in recent years and is currently 15% (from April 1995); it is almost always deducted from the gross mortgage repayments made to the lender, so that you only pay the net interest each month on the first £30,000 of your mortgage. The lender gets the rest back from the Inland Revenue.

EXAMPLE

Ann has a loan of £40,000; this month her gross repayment is £400. How much will she pay after tax relief?

Only the first £30,000 is eligible, so she gets relief on £300 of her total repayment of £400:

$$15\% \text{ of } £300 = £45$$

Her net repayment this month will be £355.

— Types of mortgage repayments —

The most common types are:

- Capital and interest
- Endowment policy
- Pension contract
- PEP mortgages

Types of mortgages	Monthly payments	Features	Advantages	Disadvantages
Capital and interest mortgages (repayment mortgages)	Cheapest	Pay off loan over a fixed term, often 25 years	As long as you keep up the payments, you will pay off the loan by the end of the term	
Endowment mortgages	More expensive	Pay interest to the lender, and also insurance premiums on an endowment policy	Varies with type of policy; you might make a profit on the policy as well as paying off the mortgage	Early surrender of the policy will lose you money; low-cost endowments don't guarantee to pay off the mortgage
Pension mortgages	Most expensive	Pay interest to the lender and contributions to a personal pension scheme	You get a pension as well as paying off the mortgage	Commits you to high payments
PEP mortgages	Cheaper	Pay interest to the lender and payments into a PEP fund	You might make a profit on the PEP fund after paying off the mortgage; tax advantages	Risky – the fund may not pay off the mortgage

Fig 11.2

Capital and interest (repayment) mortgages

Until the 1980s this was the most popular way of repaying a mortgage. As the borrower, you were notified of the regular (usually monthly) repayments you would have to make to the lender over an agreed period of time (typically 25 years). This method is regaining popularity at the expense of endowment mortgages, which were popular in the 1980s and are now increasingly being seen as expensive.

With repayment mortgages, part of each repayment is used to pay the interest on the loan, and the rest is used to repay part of the amount you borrowed. In the early years of a repayment mortgage, the largest part of the repayment goes to pay the interest, so the loan itself is paid off very slowly indeed. For example, after ten years of a 25-year repayment mortgage it is unlikely that you will have repaid much more than 10% of the original loan. In the later years, more and more of each repayment goes to repay the outstanding capital, and the amount of interest payable reduces.

Life assurance policies with capital and interest mortgages

Most lenders insist on, or at least strongly advise you to get, life cover so that a mortgage may be repaid when you die. This protects the interests of anyone you leave behind if you die as well as the interest of the lender. As the outstanding amount you have borrowed reduces each year, you progressively need less insurance to repay it, so the most appropriate life policy is a 'decreasing term assurance policy'. Although the premiums remain the same throughout, the level of death benefit reduces each year, roughly in line with the expected reduction in the loan.

Endowment mortgages

With endowment mortgages you only pay the lender the interest on the loan, but make no regular payment to reduce the outstanding loan itself. Thus the amount you initially borrow should neither increase or decrease during the mortgage term. In order to repay the loan, you take out an endowment policy to repay the loan at the end of the agreed period. You pay the premiums, and when the policy matures, the loan is repaid, but this depends on the investment performance of the policy.

There are many types of endowment policy; they are all types of 'whole of life' insurance (see Chapter 9, page 131). There is no doubt that they were 'oversold' during the 1980s; as we saw in Chapter 9, this kind of insurance does what it is supposed to do if you keep it until the end of term. What you should never do, particularly in the early years, is surrender the policy, because the surrender value will be very low or non-existent. With endowment mortgages this would be a serious problem, because you are relying on the value of the policy to pay off the mortgage.

A 1989 National Consumer Council survey found that 25% of people with endowment mortgages had cashed in their policies and taken out new ones when they moved house, when they could have simply 'topped-up' their existing policy, avoiding the problem of poor surrender values. They were poorly advised – to repeat the point:

- Keep your endowment policy until the end of its term – don't cash it in early.
- A low-cost endowment policy assumes a certain level of annual growth necessary to repay the loan at the end of the mortgage term; if that rate of growth is not achieved, then the cash at maturity will not be enough to repay the loan fully.
- Mortgages based on a full (with or without profits) endowment policy do guarantee that the original capital will be repaid.

Pension mortgages

These operate in a very similar way to endowment mortgages in that you only pay the interest on the loan to the lender, and make no repayment of the capital. The capital is eventually repaid from a pension policy. A pension mortgage is the most expensive type of mortgage in terms of what you repay monthly, in spite of the favourable tax treatment that pensions get, but it will pay you a residual pension after you have paid back the mortgage.

It is often not enough to take out a pension contract to produce a fund only just sufficient to repay the mortgage; with personal pensions, for example, only 25% of the eventual fund may be taken as a tax-free lump sum, which means that a fund four times bigger than the mortgage must be achieved if the loan is to be repaid in full, when the pension benefits are taken.

The Inland Revenue requires that pension policies should be taken out primarily as a way of saving for retirement; they should not be sold primarily as a way of repaying a mortgage.

PEP mortgages

These have become increasingly popular; they are based on the principle of making regular interest-only payments, and repaying the mortgage loan from a separate fund such as a PEP or a unit trust or investment trust savings scheme.

PEP mortgages are the cheapest kind of interest-only mortgage, but they are the most risky, because they are tied closely to the stock market. To reduce the risk, lenders tend to want the PEP fund to be invested in unit trusts rather than directly in shares.

Interest options

There is quite a variety of interest options to choose from.

- Fixed rate mortgages – these give you certainty about your monthly payments for an agreed period (usually five years) by fixing the interest you pay on the loan. There is usually an arrangement fee for this.
- Variable rate mortgage – these are where you pay the 'going rate' of interest. People got caught in the late 1980s when interest rates increased quickly and thus put up their repayments unexpectedly. In the last few years, interest rates have been low.
- Low start mortgages – these are designed to help you to keep your repayments as low as possible in the first few years, and to pay more later. This is done by not demanding any repayment of the capital at first.
- Capped and collared mortgages – these are variable-rate mortgages with fixed upper and lower limits of interest, which give you a degree of certainty about the cost of your repayments
- Deferred interest mortgages – these are the opposite of low start mortgages. In the early years you pay back the capital but not the interest. For it to work, you need to be fairly sure that you are going to be earning more in the future and the value of the house is going to go up.
- Discounted mortgages – these give a discount on the variable interest rate for a certain period. They are usually designed to attract first-time buyers.

A lot of people try to be too clever about the interest payments; the 'bottom line' is that you will have to pay interest, and whatever scheme you choose there will probably be times when you are paying more than someone else with a different scheme.

Which type of mortgage should you have?

Repayment mortgages are safe, boring and back in fashion. Other mortgages are a bit more exciting, because they hold out a promise of extra benefits. When the economy is booming, the prospect of actually getting these benefits seems realistic. When the economy is contracting, people have trouble making their monthly payments, and things look bad. This is all part of the cyclical nature of all economies (not just the UK's). Lenders understand all this perfectly well – it is everyone else who gets confused. Whichever mortgage you decide to have, your primary objective should be to make sure that you are going to be able to pay it back without having a desperate struggle. This means not borrowing too much, and being realistic about your future income – it may also mean living in a smaller place than you would like for a few years.

Cost of mortgages

If you decide not to have life cover, the cheapest type of mortgage is the repayment mortgage, followed in ascending order of expense by:

- a PEP mortgage (whose advantage over an endowment mortgage is its tax-exempt status)
- a low-cost endowment mortgage
- a personal pension mortgage (even after taking into account tax relief on the contributions).

Flexibility of the term

You can easily reduce the term of a repayment mortgage, although it is notionally fixed at the outset, by increasing your regular payments. This increases the speed of repayment of the capital, and so reduces the term. Conversely, if you reduce the regular repayments (preferably with the permission of the lender) you would automatically increase the term of the mortgage.

The term of an endowment mortgage is more difficult to change, although not so difficult as is often imagined. If you increase the payments under the endowment policy, with the permission of the insurance company, it will have a similar effect to increased repayments under a repayment mortgage. Increased premiums to the investment element of either a PEP (subject to current limits) or a pension mortgage will also have a similar effect on the term. Suppose that a few years after you have bought a house you start to earn more money, but you don't want to move. This would be a good time to start increasing your monthly repayments.

Partial repayment

Suppose you have an outstanding mortgage of £50,000 and you want to repay £3,000 of it as a lump sum.

- If you have a repayment mortgage, you simply send it to the lender and the loan will be reduced, as will the interest charges (although some lenders only apply this reduction on a fixed date each year). If you keep repaying the mortgage at the same amount as you have been previously, a greater part of the repayment will go towards paying off capital, so the loan will be paid more quickly than before.
- If you have an interest-only mortgage, the procedure is not really so different – the lump sum repayment will still reduce the amount outstanding and the interest charge. However, the term of the loan will not be changed by reducing the outstanding balance.
- With a personal pension mortgage, the reduced balance may mean that the accumulated fund may be enough to repay the loan earlier then you originally planned, although you will have to have reached the age of 50.

What if you are made redundant?

If you are made redundant the flexibility of a repayment will be important.

- With repayment mortgages the lender may be willing to defer some or all of the regular repayments almost indefinitely. Interest which you haven't paid is added to the outstanding balance of the mortgage. Remember, though, that certain social security payments may continue to meet the interest portion of your repayments.
- Under an endowment mortgage there is not likely to be quite so much flexibility, although the lender may defer repayment of interest payments if they are not paid by social security benefits. You are likely to have less flexibility in missing or deferring the endowment premiums, because most insurance companies allow a relatively short time during which you can miss paying the premiums. If you miss too many premiums, the policy will be made paid up or surrendered.

- Pension mortgages may be more flexible than endowment mortgages; more flexibility of premium payments is usually allowed with these policies, although not to the extent of repayment mortgages.
- Other interest-only mortgages such as PEP mortgages are usually similar to repayment mortgages, where a scheme gives the flexibility to amend regular contributions with little or no penalty.

Insuring against redundancy

Many lenders and advisers can arrange insurance against the cost of your mortgage repayments for a time (typically one or two years) if you are made redundant. For most people in relatively secure jobs the premium is rather high.

Protecting your mortgage

It is a good idea to ensure that your mortgage repayments are protected if you become ill or die.

- Many lenders don't require you to take out life cover for the amount of the mortgage. Even if the lender does not insist upon it, it is a good idea to take out suitable life insurance.
- Statistically, you are much more likely to suffer an illness or accident which prevents you from working for a long time than you are to die during the mortgage term. Although various social security benefits would help to some extent, you can take out insurance to cover the mortgage payments, usually for a fixed maximum of one or two years.

Using your equity

'Equity' is the difference between the value of your house and how much you have borrowed. It is the part of the value of the house that belongs to you. If you did not have a mortgage, you would have 100% equity in your house. It can be very tempting if you are a home owner to borrow money against the equity in you home. People often find themselves in a position where they have equity in a house, but no cash. Here are some common reasons why people borrow against their equity.

- Starting a business
- Paying off debts
- Paying for school fees
- Going on holiday

Borrowing against equity	Features	Advantages	Disadvantages
Further advance from your existing lender	Loan is added to your existing mortgage	Often the cheapest method	Extra charges; restrictions on the amount you borrow; restrictions on what you use the money for
Remortgage	Your original mortgage is moved to another lender, who advances you a larger one	You may be more free to do what you like with the money	Extra charges
Second mortgage	A loan secured on your property 'sits on top' of the first loan	Often completely free to do what you like with the money	Higher interest rate (usually); lenders less tolerant if you have trouble making payments

Fig 11.3

Suppose you own a home worth £100,000 and a mortgage of £60,000; you therefore have equity of £40,000. Perhaps this represents more money than you have ever actually had in cash at any one time in your life. Why shouldn't you spend some of that money? It's yours, isn't it?

Before examining how to borrow against equity, here are a few arguments for and against doing so.

- Any loan you raise in this way will be secured against your house – this means that it is relatively easy for the lender to cause your home to be repossessed if you miss repayments. Lenders of this kind of loan are generally less tolerant than the lender of your main mortgage.
- Consider how you are going to use the money: couldn't you save up for the thing you want?
- In times of high inflation, it may make good sense to borrow against equity if its proportion is high, because of gearing (see page 69).

Why is borrowing against equity so attractive?

Basically because it is so comparatively easy to do it. A lender who would refuse you the money on an unsecured basis, on the grounds that there is an unacceptably high risk that you cannot repay the loan satisfactorily, might well agree to a loan secured on your house. As we saw in Chapter 6, an important criterion for making unsecured loans is the level of your income and how secure it is. This is because the lender expects to be repaid out of your income. In the case of secured loans, however, although still wanting to see that you will be able to repay the loan out of your income, the lender is less worried and knows that if you fail to repay, your house can be sold to recover the money that way. Knowing this, the lender feels safer, and is more likely to lend you the money. In fact, the security which you are offering will often mean you will be able to get the loan at a lower rate of interest.

Getting a further advance from the existing lender

Probably the most convenient way of releasing equity from one's home – and often the cheapest way – is to apply to your existing lender for a further advance. The existing loan will remain intact, and if the lender agrees to the loan this new advance may be effected over the remaining term of the initial loan (usually) or over some other period. There will be expenses – usually a survey of the house, and, less frequently, an arranged fee.

Remortgages

Many lenders have quite strict guidelines on what propositions they will and will not consider for further advances – for example, quite a number will not give advances unless the money is being used for home improvements. Often the maximum total loan (including the original loan) may be restricted to a percentage of the value of the property (say 85%).

Other lenders have less restrictive lending criteria and so if you are refused a further advance from your own lender, you could seek to move you entire borrowings from your existing lender to a different source of finance. This process is called a 'remortgage' and usually consists of the new lender taking over your existing mortgage and advancing a further sum of money. The costs involved in a remortgage are usually higher then those for a further advance. There will be:

- a valuation fee
- solicitors' fees
- an arrangement fee.

These charges make this option unattractive for small further advances (say under £5,000). If you arrange a remortgage to help re-finance other debts, such as credit cards and personal loans, on which you are paying high rates of interest, then it may be worthwhile in the long term.

Secured second mortgages

Most banks and building societies will try to establish that:

- you can meet the regular repayments on your loan.
- you have a clean credit history (i.e. no County Court Judgements for bad debts).
- the security in the house will cover the loan.
- the reason for borrowing further money meets their criteria (e.g. home improvement only).

Usually they carry out quite comprehensive investigations to make sure that your situation does fit their rules. Lenders in the second mortgage market usually operate to less strict rules; they provide a second loan that 'sits on top' of the main mortgage.

EXAMPLE

Your house is worth £100,000
Your mortgage is £60,000
Your equity is therefore £40,000

If you take out a second mortgage with a different lender for, say, £20,000, the picture will look like this:

EXAMPLE

Your house is worth £100,000
Your main mortgage is £60,00
Your second mortgage is £20,000
Your equity is therefore £20,000

If you default on your loan repayments and the lenders repossess the house and sell it, the main lender would get their money back first, and the second lender would be paid out of what was left. Suppose, for example, your house was repossessed and sold quickly for £90,000 after costs (you would have trouble preventing the lenders from doing this):

EXAMPLE

Sale of house £90,000
First lender £60,000
Second lender £20,000
Your equity £10,000

In this case you would get some equity back, but less than if you had had the freedom to sell the house in your own time.

Often second mortgage lenders do not want to know the reason you are borrowing the money – there are usually no arrangement, valuation or legal fees but the interest rate charged will be comparatively high. The reason why they don't want to know why you are borrowing is because they aren't going to be very patient if you default, unlike your first mortgage lender who will generously bend over backwards to help if you are in trouble, and therefore wants to stop you borrowing unwisely.

Conclusions

The secret of the successful use of mortgages is not to borrow more than you can afford. As long as you keep up the payments, you will eventually own your own home.

12

—— RUNNING A CAR ——

What have cars got to do with money management? Anyone who has had a car will know just how significant an item of expense they are, and how difficult it can be to estimate and control the costs of keeping a car on the road. In this chapter we will concentrate on second-hand cars, which, if you buy them wisely, are the cheapest and most cost-effective kind of vehicle. You do not have to mechanically minded to buy and run a car economically.

Do you need a car?

Many people seriously underestimate the costs of car ownership, and lurch from one car crisis to the next. Often it is hard to look at cars rationally – we easily get caught up in ideas about the social status of particular makes and models, and what a car says about our personality.

From the point of view of money management, too much concern about the fashion aspect of car ownership can be a big mistake – it can cost you a lot of money, in ways you might not expect. The motor trade knows all about how to play on people's psychological weaknesses.

If you really do need a car it will usually be for one or more of the following reasons.

- Getting to work or college
- Cost-effective shopping
- Having an active social life
- Developing your career
- Looking after others

Buying a car	Minimum likely annual running cost	Minimum likely annual depreciation	Insurance	Repairs and servicing	Should you join a motoring organisation?
If you are experienced	£1,000	£300 – £500	Lower if you have few accidents and have been driving for a long time	Do simple jobs yourself	Worthwhile if you take long trips
If you are not experienced	£1,000	£300 – £1,000	High if you are young, haven't been driving for long, and/or drive a fast car	Get a friend to show you how to do simple maintenance	Probably a good idea

Fig 12.1

The costs of keeping a used car on the road

Once you have bought a car, the main costs of keeping it on the road are:

- insurance
- MOT
- vehicle tax (road tax)
- fuel
- repairs and servicing
- motoring organisation membership.

Insurance

Car insurance was covered in some detail in Chapter 9, Insurance (see page 115). The main points are:

- By law you cannot drive a car on a public road without having third-party insurance.
- Most people also insure their own cars against theft and damage as well.

The cost of insuring a car depends on a wide range of factors (see pages 122), over most of which you don't have much control; you can't change your age, for example, except by growing older. The factor over which you have most control is the type of car you purchase. Fuel-injected and turbo-charged engines can increase your insurance premiums massively. If you buy a car with a small engine and you are not yourself in a high-risk category, the cheapest third-party insurance is still going to cost you in the region of £150 pounds a year.

Ministry of Transport test certificate (MOT)

After a car is three years old, or has been registered for three years, it has to pass an MOT test each year. It is against the law to drive a car of 'testable age' on a public road without a valid MOT, except in certain cases such as driving it to an MOT station to be tested. Your insurance will probably be invalid if the car does not have a valid MOT. The MOT test is quite a comprehensive check on whether many parts of the car are functioning – it is not, however, a guarantee of roadworthiness. To have the car tested, you take it to an authorised garage and pay a fee. After the test you will be given a list of the items tested and what has been found.

If the car fails the test, you can either leave it at the garage for repairs, in which case a retest will be free, or, if the items on which the car failed are minor, you have a day in which to repair them before getting a free retest. If the faults are not so minor, but you don't want the testing garage to do the repairs (for example because the garage is expensive), you will have to pay for another test. The test fee is currently £27.38 (1995/96). Some garages offer discounts as a loss leader to encourage you to use them for repairs.

Vehicle licence (road tax)

By law, every car has to have a valid vehicle licence to be driven on a public road. It is a piece of round printed paper (the disc) which is displayed on the windscreen. You can buy your disc at a post office, or send off for it by post using an appropriate form. A six-month disc currently costs £77 (1995/96) and a one-year disc currently costs £140. If you have the cash, it is more economic to buy the one-year disc.

Fuel

Diesel is becoming more popular as a fuel for private cars because it can give up to 25% more efficiency than petrol, and is also a little cheaper to buy. You have to use a car with a diesel engine; second-hand models are harder to find and relatively more expensive than petrol models. Most people, however, will have a petrol car. Older cars may have to use leaded petrol, which is more expensive than the environmentally friendly unleaded petrol. The amount of fuel your car uses depends on:

- The size of the engine
- The mechanical condition of the car
- How much you drive the car
- Whether you use it mostly for long journeys or short ones

Smaller-engine cars tend to use less fuel. Frequent short journeys in traffic use more fuel per mile than taking longer journeys on open roads. Fuel is a major cost of having a car; with experience, you can estimate how much it will cost you personally, based on your own car-using habits. Someone who uses their car fairly frequently can spend at least £500 a year on fuel without taking many long journeys.

Repairs and servicing

If you can learn the basics of servicing a car, or have a friend who will do it for nothing, you will save money and prolong the life of the vehicle. The annual cost of repairs can vary enormously; this is where garages make their money. If, like me, you are not mechanically minded, it is very easy to pay over the odds for repairs. The way to keep the cost of repairs down is:

- Buy a mechanically sound example of a reliable make and model – get a knowledgeable friend to help you do this.
- Service your car regularly.
- Develop a network of trusted friends and mechanics who know about cars and can advise and/or do the repairs cheaply.

Even minor accidents can be expensive to repair. If you bump into someone else's car and it is your fault, it may be cheaper to agree to pay for the repairs to their vehicle than to make an insurance claim which will increase your insurance premiums in future years. The annual MOT test will probably also entail paying for repairs. If you are not mechanically minded, but drive a reliable car and get good value for repairs, you are still likely to spend at least £200 a year on repairs, and this figure may be much higher.

Motoring organisation membership

These organisations, including the AA, RAC and National Breakdown Service, offer a variety of breakdown services in return for an annual fee. If you use motorways, take long journeys, or have an unreliable car, membership will probably pay for itself. This is because the costs of being towed or having emergency repairs can be very high. If you only use your car locally and it is reliable, it may make sense to save money by not taking out membership. It depends on the type of membership you buy, but you can expect an annual cost of about £100.

Summary of running costs

If you are a reasonably frequent car user with an economical and reliable car which you mainly use locally, the minimum cost of running the car each year is likely to be:

Third party insurance	£150
MOT	£27.38
Road tax	£140
Fuel	£500
Repairs and servicing	£200
Motoring organisation membership	–
Total	£1,017.38

For many people this would be a very optimistic figure. If you are inexperienced or have a more expensive car, your true annual running costs can easily be £3,000 or more.

Depreciation

Another item which should be added to your estimate of the running costs is the cost of depreciation. We have just seen that the annual running costs of a car will be at least £1,000 for most people. In some cases, this will be more than you actually paid to buy the car. Unless you are in the trade, your car is not going to make you money. It is going to cost you money. When you buy a car, don't overestimate its likely resale value when it is time to sell it; the difference between the price you pay for the car and the price at which you sell it represents a loss. Dividing the number of years you own the car by the loss you make when you sell it gives you its annual depreciation figure.

EXAMPLE

You buy a car for £3,000 and sell it after five years for £800. What is the annual depreciation?

- Work out the total loss   £3,000–£800 = £2,200
- Divide the loss by the number of years you owned the car   £2,200 ÷ 5 = £440

The annual depreciation has been £440.

While you don't know what the exact depreciation figure will be, you can estimate it from price guides in handbooks and magazines available in newsagents. Add your estimate of the depreciation figure to your estimate of the annual running costs; this brings the total annual costs in the example on page 195 to nearly £1,500.

You may well find that your depreciation figure is higher – you are choosing the car you need now which is the best you can afford, but you probably don't know when you are going to sell it, so it is difficult to predict accurately what the resale price will be. In general cars which depreciate slowly are those which are subject to import restrictions (some Japanese cars, for example) and cars which are popular, such as the BMW 300 series. Unpopular models may depreciate much more quickly, but can be very good value because of their reliability.

Two strategies

Depreciation is an ongoing battle. As a general rule, buying a car which is more than three years old will avoid the large losses on all new cars; if you then sell it after a further three years and before any major repairs, you should be able to keep your running costs and depreciation costs stable and predictable. This approach means that you have to pay a high price to buy the car.

Another strategy is to buy a reliable car which is much older and cheaper and either run it until you sell it for scrap or sell it at near the price it cost you. For example, under £1,000, car prices can sometimes stabilise for several years. If you buy a car for £1,000 or less, your annual depreciation is likely to be between £300 and £500, but could be less than £200.

Used car price guides

These are very useful, both for estimating depreciation and for giving you a rough guide to the current price of the car you want, whether you are buying privately, through a dealer or by auction. They are also useful for pricing your car when you come to sell it. As well as the price guides in motoring magazines, handbooks include:

- Parker's Price Guide
- The Motorists' Guide
- The Motor Trade Guide to Used Car Prices
- Greenlight's Used Car Prices.

These guides also contain other useful information on insurance, market reports and the makes and models of vehicles.

Summary

With the true cost of car ownership at least £1,500 a year, it represents a major item of expenditure in your household budget. Good maintenance and planning will help you minimise the running costs, which are the most variable and hard-to-control element in the overall cost. Many people really do need a car in their lives, but it is worth considering not having one, or having a cheap one. From a financial point of view, wouldn't it be nice to be putting the £1,500 into a pension or savings account instead? Remember that a car is rarely an investment – it is a cost of living which you spend, and don't get back, like buying food. Take trouble over buying and maintaining your car, and make friends with people who know about cars – it will save you hundreds, if not thousands, of pounds a year. If you use the car on long journeys, become a member of a motoring organisation; the money you save on one breakdown a year away from home can easily cover the cost of membership.

13

—— **DEALING WITH** ——
DEBT

If we were computers instead of human beings, we might never get into debt – but as human beings, however sensible we may be normally, crises and big life changes can affect us emotionally. Bereavement, a dramatic love affair, divorce and illness, to name only a few, can sometimes cause us to behave carelessly with money, only to come to our senses some time later and to be faced with a pile of debts.

Record numbers of people have got into debt in the UK in the last few years, courtesy of a credit boom in the 1980s. Credit booms – an economic process by which it becomes easier for people to borrow money – encourage everyone to borrow more than they should. If you are in debt now, the chances are that your bad habits started in the late 1980s.

You are not going to get out of debt by ignoring your creditors. The problem doesn't just go away, and you risk being taken to court, with all the stress and worry that entails. The only way to avoid this is to negotiate and communicate!

Some debtors become expert at running away, and use great skill and imagination in evading their pursuers. Such people come from all backgrounds and walks of life: students, plumbers, solicitors, managers – even some Oxbridge dons – have become 'professional' debtors. As a way of life it has little to recommend it, so it is assumed here that you will not want to 'go professional', or even become a highly talented amateur, in the defaulting game.

If you are in debt, it is quite likely that a large proportion of it is made up of bank loans and credit cards. An important thing to realise is that these institutions expect a proportion of their customers to default – one reason why the rates of interest they charge are high. Credit cards in particular have high interest charges because almost anyone is allowed to borrow, making the risk of default high.

Big banks and finance houses are accustomed to having to chase their bad debts with nasty letters and legal action. They also know that if the debt is unsecured, they are likely to receive only a fraction of what they have lent if they sue you or you become bankrupt. If, on the other hand, they can arrange a repayment schedule with you, they are more likely to get most of the money back.

If you make a clean breast of your problems, creditors, whether secured or unsecured, are much more likely to deal fairly and leniently with you – not only do they know that they are more likely to get their money back this way, but they are also under pressure to do so from the government and from their own need for a good public image. Get on friendly terms with the individuals who you are dealing with, and note their names.

Rent arrears

Rent arrears are very common, particularly with council housing, and many councils adopt a sympathetic attitude towards tenants who have fallen into arrears through financial difficulties. You should contact your housing officer or estate manager if you fall into arrears; it may be possible to repay these through a small addition to your regular rental payments. If the arrears are large and you can plead your case effectively, you may even be able to have them written off altogether.

You can also seek help from a Citizen's Advice Bureau, Housing Aid Centre or even your MP. Another possibility is to exchange your flat with another council tenant who has a cheaper one.

If you are in arrears with a private landlord, that person or company is likely to move very promptly to recover the money or to have you evicted for non-payment. You must be very careful to communicate with the landlord and try to reach an agreement for repayment. You might, for example, be able to negotiate on the basis of some repairs which need to be done – perhaps you could exchange your labour or materials for a reduction in the arrears.

If you persist in failing to pay the rent, whether in the private or public sector, you will inevitably at some stage receive a notice to quit, followed by a court summons if no agreement can be reached. This summons will include a 'form of admission' which you should complete and return to the court. The form will contain a section allowing you to plead your case.

Arrears of unsecured loans

You must find out the name of the person to write to, and tell them that:

- you fully intend to pay your outstanding debt
- you have a plan to repay your debt
- all your creditors will be repaid an amount proportionate to your outstanding debt
- you can afford to pay £X monthly
- in the case of interest-bearing debt, ask them to 'freeze' it, that is, not charge further interest.

Most creditors will respond by accepting your offer. (Remember that this will save them a lot of time and expense in chasing you.) If they refuse to freeze the debt, try to persuade them to reduce the rate of interest paid on the outstanding balance. Some creditors will continue to pressurise you to pay more – but they are on stickier legal ground if you have written to them as outlined above, and you should resist them, continuing to pay a regular monthly amount sent to a named person at the company. Remember to keep copies of all correspondence.

It will help convince creditors that you are serious if you supply the names and addresses of other creditors who have accepted your repayment plan. The fact that other companies are going along with your repayment plan will reassure them that you are not trying to deceive them.

Writing a letter to a creditor

If you find it difficult to sit down and write to your creditors, try a version of the following letter.

Your name
Your street
Your town
Your county
Your postcode
Tel. 0000 000

The date

The name of your contact

Credit company name

Address

Dear (contact name),

I am writing to you to let you know that I have been finding it increasingly difficult to meet my monthly repayments on my loan (reference number).

I have recently decided to put my financial affairs in order, and to start a programme of strict budgeting, with the help of Mr XYZ of the XYZ Citizen's Advice Bureau. According to this budget, I have identified the amount of money which I can afford to repay your company each month. This is the sum of £X.

I have a number of other creditors, all of whom are receiving payments in proportion to the amount of money I owe them. If you require it, I can supply you with their names and addresses.

If my income increases in the future, I will be able to increase the repayments.

I would be very grateful if you would freeze the sum outstanding at its present level, so that I can repay it within a reasonable time.

Thank you for your help in this matter.

Yours sincerely

Your name

This kind of letter really works. It protects you in various legal ways and it tells the creditors what they want to know.

What if you end up in court?

Some people reading this book may already be so far down the road to chronic debt that they are being threatened by creditors with court action. If this is happening, don't panic! No-one is going to send you to prison or to the workhouse! Contact your creditors immediately and try to negotiate a realistic repayment schedule. Use professional help if necessary.

The great point about being taken to court is that your side of the story is taken into account. If you can produce copies of your letters offering to repay according to a schedule, and the magistrate believes that you are acting in good faith (which he or she almost certainly will if you are), you are likely to be ordered to repay to the schedule you have proposed. If you have not proposed a schedule, the magistrate will ask you to do so or, if the creditor does not agree with it, set one himself.

A word of warning – the court can make life difficult for you if you don't stick to the agreed schedule, so make sure that the regular amount you have offered to repay is truly realistic – err on the low side.

The Small Claims Court

This is the simplest way of suing someone for repayment of a debt – there is an upper limit on the amount you can sue for. A claim form is submitted to the court and a summons is issued to the debtor; if you do not respond to the summons, a judgement is automatically made against you. The best way of dealing with a Small Claims summons is to respond in detail when you receive it, offering a repayment schedule. Sometimes creditors ask for more than you really owe when responding to the summons.

Bailiffs

There are people who never pay their bills, and the law provides a centuries-old remedy to deal with them – the bailiff. If you follow the procedures outlined earlier you should never have to suffer a visit from a bailiff. In the last few years, however, there have been disturbing reports of an increasing number of cases of 'bully boy' tactics being used on debtors who are not adept at dealing with their creditors. Bailiffs, or people claiming to be bailiffs, have deceived debtors and exceeded their powers in attempting to recover debts. Here's what a bailiff with a warrant is allowed to do.

Appear at your front door without warning
Use 'reasonable force' to effect an entry
Take away goods belonging to the debtor

A bailiff cannot take away goods that are not wholly owned by the debtor (except in exceptional circumstances). Goods bought on hire purchase, for instance, cannot normally be taken away, if you produce documents to prove their ownership. If a bailiff knocks on your door, *before* you let him in, ask to see identification and a distress warrant, and read them. If there is no warrant, or the debtor concerned does not live at the address, don't let them in (make a note of their names, though – they may not actually be bailiffs).

Legitimate creditors will not send in the bailiffs without good reason, but some have been using bailiffs to scare debtors into paying sooner than they might.

A confrontation with a bailiff can be a nasty, scary experience; often they are scared too (you might be an axe murderer for all they know), which makes them aggressive. Keep your head, and behave firmly. If you know they are in the right, you will have to let them take your possessions – normally they are only interested in things like furniture, TVs, videos and washing machines which can be resold.

Attachment of earnings orders

These orders only apply to people who are in stable employment. They are often used to ensure that people pay such things as child maintenance or council tax. Your employer is required to deduct the necessary amount directly from your wages and pay it to the court. The court will then pay your creditors. Note, however, that your employer is under no legal obligation to cooperate with the order – so discuss the matter with your employer and find another way to repay the debt.

Bankruptcy

Bankruptcy is a precise term, but is often confused with other forms of insolvency, such as the winding up of a company. Only an individual (not a company) can become bankrupt, and only a court can make a person bankrupt.

The days of bankruptcy as a horrific social stigma may be over, but it is still a state to be avoided at almost all costs. During the recession years of the early 1990s there were record numbers of bankruptcies, and most people probably know one or two bankrupts personally. Of the 20 or so bankrupts known personally to me, there is only one who I believe 'had' to go bankrupt – he owes more than £20 million and is in his late 60s, so he is not going to be able to offer a realistic repayment schedule to his creditors. All the others could, and probably should, have avoided bankruptcy by making arrangements with their creditors early – usually they had been running a small business for which they were personally liable (they could have limited their liability by using a limited company), were inexperienced businesspeople and had borrowed too much money. The problem is that when a person has reached the point when bankruptcy is looming, they are too upset and stressed to be able to study their options carefully.

Bankruptcy is very much a last resort for a debtor, although it is often entered into voluntarily. Once bankrupted, you are unable to lead a normal life for a minimum of two years and sometimes longer. During this period you will have little income to live on, even if you are earning a good salary, because most of the money will go to your creditors. Your family life will probably suffer, and you are likely to lose your home.

Bankruptcy usually occurs when debts are more than £750 and the debtor cannot pay. The creditor will have issued a statutory demand against the debtor, who then has 21 days in which to decide whether to apply to have the demand set aside. There are various grounds for having demands set aside, such as if the debtor has a counter-claim against the creditor, or there are other reasonable grounds for dispute. If the statutory demand is not set aside, then the creditor is allowed to serve a bankruptcy petition on the debtor. This is followed by a court hearing, at which point there is still time for an agreement to be made between the debtor and creditor which enables bankruptcy to be avoided.

Alternatively, a debtor can also present a petition to the court in order to declare voluntary bankruptcy. Whatever the source of the petition, once bankruptcy has been declared, the official receiver takes charge of all assets belonging to the bankrupt except for essential tools of the trade, clothing and bedding.

Once bankrupted, a person lives a financially controlled life. He or she can only have a bank account with the permission of the court, and this will not have a cheque card or overdraft facility. Any property belonging to the bankrupt will be sold within a year, although if it is in joint names the partner should be entitled to 50% of the proceeds. The bankrupt will live more or less at subsistence level for two years, which is the normal period of bankruptcy for people whose estates (total assets) are valued at less than £20,000.

Conclusion

The hardest part of dealing with debt is psychological: you have to face up to your situation before you can do anything positive about it. Never despair; our society does not force anyone to suffer for the rest of their lives because of debt, so long as honest attempts are made to repay creditors. By following the procedures outlined in this chapter, you will eventually be able to satisfy your debts ad get back on your financial feet.

APPENDIX

To help you get into the budgeting habit, here are some blank budget forms which you can use for your annual and monthly accounts.

Last year's expenditure   Date:

Accommodation (mortgage or rent)   £

Food (including restaurants, school dinners,
    motorway sandwiches)   £

Household consumables (things you buy for the
    house, such as detergents, garden and hoover bags)   £

Bills
- Telephone   £
- Electricity   £
- Gas   £
- Oil   £
- Solid fuel   £
- Council tax   £
- Water rates   £
- TV licence   £
- Equipment rental and HP   £

Insurance
- Buildings insurance   £
- Contents insurance   £

Car
- Car insurance   £
- Fuel   £
- Repairs and servicing   £

- Road tax and MOT £
- Loss of value (this is called 'depreciation' – for information on how to calculate depreciation see Chapter 12). £
- AA/RAC membership £

Other transport (including trains, buses and taxis) £

Savings and investment £
- TESSA £
- PEPS £
- Bank/building society deposits £
- SAYE £
- Life insurance £
- Pension £
- Other £

House maintenance £

Holiday
- Travel £
- Hotels £
- Spending money £

Other personal items
- Cigarettes £
- Alcohol (include what you spend in pubs) £
- Theatre/cinema/video £
- Sports and hobbies £
- Newspapers, magazines, audio cassettes £
- Clothes £
- Other £

Miscellaneous
- Furniture £
- Pet food and vet fees £
- Borrowings £
- Other £
- Bank interest and charges £

Tax, if not taken at source £

Total expenditure £

Last year's income £

Your total income after tax, from all sources, including state benefits £

Next year's expenditure   Date:

Accommodation (mortgage or rent)   £

Food (including restaurants, school dinners,
    motorway sandwiches)   £

Household consumables (things you buy for the
    house, such as detergents, garden and hoover bags)   £

Bills
- Telephone   £
- Electricity   £
- Gas   £
- Oil   £
- Solid fuel   £
- Council tax   £
- Water rates   £
- TV licence   £
- Equipment rental and HP   £

Insurance
- Buildings insurance   £
- Contents insurance   £

Car
- Car insurance   £
- Fuel   £
- Repairs and servicing   £
- Road tax and MOT   £
- Loss of value (this is called 'depreciation' – for
    information on how to calculate depreciation
    see Chapter 12).   £
- AA/RAC membership   £

Other transport (including trains, buses and taxis)   £

Savings and investment   £
- TESSA   £
- PEPS   £
- Bank/building society deposits   £
- SAYE   £
- Life insurance   £
- Pension   £
- Other   £

House maintenance   £

Holiday
- Travel £
- Hotels £
- Spending money £

Other personal items
- Cigarettes £
- Alcohol (include what you spend in pubs) £
- Theatre/cinema/video £
- Sports and hobbies £
- Newspapers, magazines, audio cassettes £
- Clothes £
- Other £

Miscellaneous
- Furniture £
- Pet food and vet fees £
- Borrowings £
- Other £
- Bank interest and charges £

Tax, if not taken at source £

Total expenditure £

Last year's income £

**Your total income after tax, from all sources,
including state benefits** £

Last month's expenditure   Date:

Accommodation (mortgage or rent)   £

Food (including restaurants, school dinners,
     motorway sandwiches)   £

Household consumables (things you buy for the
     house, such as detergents, garden and hoover bags)   £

Bills
- Telephone   £
- Electricity   £
- Gas   £
- Oil   £
- Solid fuel   £
- Council tax   £
- Water rates   £
- TV licence   £
- Equipment rental and HP   £

Insurance
- Buildings insurance   £
- Contents insurance   £

Car
- Car insurance   £
- Fuel   £
- Repairs and servicing   £
- Road tax and MOT   £
- Loss of value (this is called 'depreciation' – for
  information on how to calculate depreciation
  see Chapter 12).   £
- AA/RAC membership   £

Other transport (including trains, buses and taxis)   £

Savings and investment   £
- TESSA   £
- PEPS   £
- Bank/building society deposits   £
- SAYE   £
- Life insurance   £
- Pension   £

- Other   £

House maintenance   £

Holiday
- Travel   £
- Hotels   £
- Spending money   £

Other personal items
- Cigarettes   £
- Alcohol (include what you spend in pubs)   £
- Theatre/cinema/video   £
- Sports and hobbies   £
- Newspapers, magazines, audio cassettes   £
- Clothes   £
- Other   £

Miscellaneous
- Furniture   £
- Pet food and vet fees   £
- Borrowings   £
- Other   £
- Bank interest and charges   £

Tax, if not taken at source   £

Total expenditure   £

Last month's income   £

**Your total income after tax, from all sources,
including state benefits**   £

Next month's expenditure   Date:

Accommodation (mortgage or rent)   £

Food (including restaurants, school dinners,
    motorway sandwiches)   £

Household consumables (things you buy for the
    house, such as detergents, garden and hoover bags)   £

Bills
- Telephone   £
- Electricity   £
- Gas   £
- Oil   £
- Solid fuel   £
- Council tax   £
- Water rates   £
- TV licence   £
- Equipment rental and HP   £

Insurance
- Buildings insurance   £
- Contents insurance   £

Car
- Car insurance   £
- Fuel   £
- Repairs and servicing   £
- Road tax and MOT   £
- Loss of value (this is called 'depreciation' – for
  information on how to calculate depreciation
  see chapter 12).   £
- AA/RAC membership   £

Other transport (including trains, buses and taxis)   £

Savings and investment   £
- TESSA   £
- PEPS   £
- Bank/building society deposits   £
- SAYE   £
- Life insurance   £
- Pension   £

- Other £

House maintenance £

Holiday
- Travel £
- Hotels £
- Spending money £

Other personal items
- Cigarettes £
- Alcohol (include what you spend in pubs) £
- Theatre/cinema/video £
- Sports and hobbies £
- Newspapers, magazines, audio cassettes £
- Clothes £
- Other £

Miscellaneous
- Furniture £
- Pet food and vet fees £
- Borrowings £
- Other £
- Bank interest and charges £

Tax, if not taken at source £

Total expenditure £

Next month's income £

Your total income after tax, from all sources, including state benefits £

USEFUL ADDRESSES

Financial Intermediaries, Managers and Brokers Regulatory
Association (FIMBRA)
Hertsmere House
Hertsmere Road
London E14 4AB
Tel. 0171 538 8860

Investment Management Regulatory Organisation (IMRO)
Broadwalk House
5 Appold House
London EC2A 2LL
Tel. 0171 628 6022

Life Assurance and Unit Trust Regulatory Organisation (LAUTRO)
Centre Point
103 New Oxford Street
London WC1A 1QH
Tel. 0171 379 0444

The National Association of Citizen's Advice Bureaux
115–123 Pentonville Road
London N1 9LZ
Tel. 0171 823 2181

Office of Fair Trading
Chancery House
53 Chancery Lane
London WC2A 1SP
Tel. 0171 242 2858

Occupational Pensions Advisory Service (OPAS)
11 Belgrave Road
London SW1V 1RB
Tel. 0171 233 8080

Personal Investment Authority (PIA)
3–4 Royal Exchange
London EC3V 3NL
Tel. 0171 929 0072

BIBLIOGRAPHY

Baker, Helen, *Money Matters for Women*. Penguin 1993.

Delderfield, Paul, *Successful Borrowing and Coping with Debt*. Daily Telegraph Publications 1987.

Gough, Leo, *Teach Yourself Choosing a Pension*. Hodder & Stoughton 1996.

Joseph, Michael, *The Conveyancing Fraud*. Micheal Joseph 1989.

Lubbock, Bill and Stokes, Richard, *How to Get a Job*. Hamlyn 1989.

Schwed, Fred, Jr *Where are the Customers' Yachts?* Simon and Schuster 1940.

Stolper, Michael, *Wealth: an Owner's Manual*. HarperBusiness 1992.

Tolley's Tax Guide. Tolley Publishing Company, annual.

Train, John, *Preserving Capital and Making It Grow*. Penguin 1993.

The Motorists' Price Guide. Foxpride, annual.

Parker's Used, New & Trade Car Price Guide. Parker Mead, annual.

Magazines

Money Management
Tel. 0171 405 6969

Occupational Pensions
Tel. 0171 354 5858

Planned Savings
Tel. 0181 868 4499

INDEX